ST. OLAF COLLEGE LIBRARIES

S0-CJQ-018

# A Double Bind: The Exclusion of Pastoralist Women in the East and Horn of Africa

By Naomi Kipuri and Andrew Ridgewell

# Contents

RECEIVED

APR 2 7 2009

ROLVAAG MEMORIAL
LIBRARY
ST. OLAF COLLEGE

# Acronyms

ABEK        Alternative Basic Education Programme for
            Karamoja (Uganda)
ALARMP      Arid Lands Resource Management Project
            (Kenya)
APDA        Afar Pastoral Development Association (Ethiopia)
CAHW        Community Animal Health Workers
CEDAW       Convention on the Elimination of all Forms of
            Discrimination Against Women
DHS         Demographic and Health Survey
EPRDF       Ethiopian People's Revolutionary Democratic
            Front
FGM         Female Genital Mutilation
FPAU        Family Planning Association of Uganda
GDP         Gross Domestic Product
ICERD       International Convention on the Elimination of all
            Forms of Racial Discrimination

KADP        Karamoja Agro-Pastoral Development
            Programme (Uganda)
NTFP        Non-Timber Forest Product
KENDA       Kenya National Democratic Alliance
KEWOPA      Kenya Women Parliamentary Association
MWEDO       Maasai Women Development Organization
            (Tanzania)
ODM         Orange Democratic Movement (Kenya)
ODM-K       Orange Democratic Movement Party of Kenya
PNU         Party of National Unity (Kenya)
PWC         Pastoral Women's Council (Tanzania)
TEV         Total Economic Value
UDM         United Democratic Movement (Kenya)
UWOPA       Uganda Women Parliamentary Association
WPDC        Wajir Peace and Development Committee
            (Kenya)

31895/290

# Executive summary

Pastoralism is the one of the predominant livelihoods of east Africa and the Horn. It contributes significantly to national economies and can conserve fragile natural resources. Yet pastoralists remain socially and economically marginalized and have little or no representation in local and national government. Governments in the region continue to hold that pastoralism is unsustainable and a barrier to development.

Despite the numerous key tasks women fulfil in pastoralist society, they face this discrimination two-fold. They are even less able than pastoralist men to participate in the decisions that affect their lives and livelihoods.

Very few women have succeeded in campaigning for an open parliamentary seat. The total number of pastoralist women MPs in Kenya, Tanzania and Uganda adds up to only a handful. In Ethiopia, which has the largest pastoralist population, there are a number of notable pastoralist women MPs, but they tend to be confined to junior positions. It is important to note that, of the four countries discussed in this report, the two that operate extensive affirmative action for women – Tanzania and Uganda – actually have the lowest number of pastoralist women parliamentarians elected by constituency, which suggests that the system has not favoured women from minority groups. Throughout the region, poor levels of political participation in Parliament are replicated at other levels of government, and concerns over pastoralist women's participation will often be overshadowed by concerns over political representation in general.

The lack of access to political participation has roots in a deeper marginalization. This report provides an analysis of mainstream attitudes towards the pastoralist way of life and of pastoralist attitudes towards women.

Little has been done to adapt education and health services to pastoralist livelihoods. Though governments may have taken steps to address the gender gap in education in general, these measures are not reaching pastoralist girls. A recent household survey in the Somali Region of Ethiopia found that the literacy rate for male pastoralists was 22.7 percent and for female pastoralists only 4.8 percent. In Kenya, statistics show that women in remote pastoralist areas are seven times more likely to give birth without antenatal care.

Pastoralist culture excludes women from important roles. Pastoralist women are brought up to respect and submit to the leadership of men. Women continue to be subject to female genital mutilation. If they do not, some consider them incapable of participating in decision-making. They are often married forcibly, or while still young, in order to maximize bridewealth payments.

The perception that pastoralism is unsustainable, as well as rapid commercialization, climate change and ongoing conflicts are forcing pastoralists into sedentarizaton. Women shoulder increasingly heavy burdens to provide for their families, which also impacts on girls' education and constrains their participation in public life.

Pastoralist women must work longer and harder than men, fulfilling 'female' roles in the household, as well as making money from tasks traditionally deemed to be 'women's work', including collecting firewood, and making and selling handicrafts. This labour is in such demand that girls are often removed from school in order to work. Women do not attend many of the social occasions at which men make decisions that affect the whole community.

Women play a central role in livestock production, the main source of income and prestige for pastoralists. Policy-makers have failed to recognize this – a factor which lies behind the shortcomings of many livestock development projects.

Climate change has also taken its toll. As drought forces men further afield with herds in search of water, women remain behind and must manage the household. Women's knowledge of the environment is crucial in these times, and yet this knowledge, along with the specific plight women face, often goes ignored in drought mitigation strategies.

As resources become increasingly scarce and conflict flares, women – seen as the mothers of future generations of 'the enemy' – are at risk of abduction, rape and murder. They also bear the burden of supporting their households in times of war. Yet their proven capacity as peace-builders does not translate into support when they seek political office. Men – the perpetrators of violence – are still seen as the natural candidates when it comes to the ballot box.

Governments and NGOs have a more active role to play in supporting and promoting pastoralist women's participation. Pastoralist women who become leaders are living examples that, by providing access to the necessary skills, experiences and knowledge, pastoralist women can address the constraints on their participation themselves.

# Ethiopia, Kenya, Tanzania and Uganda

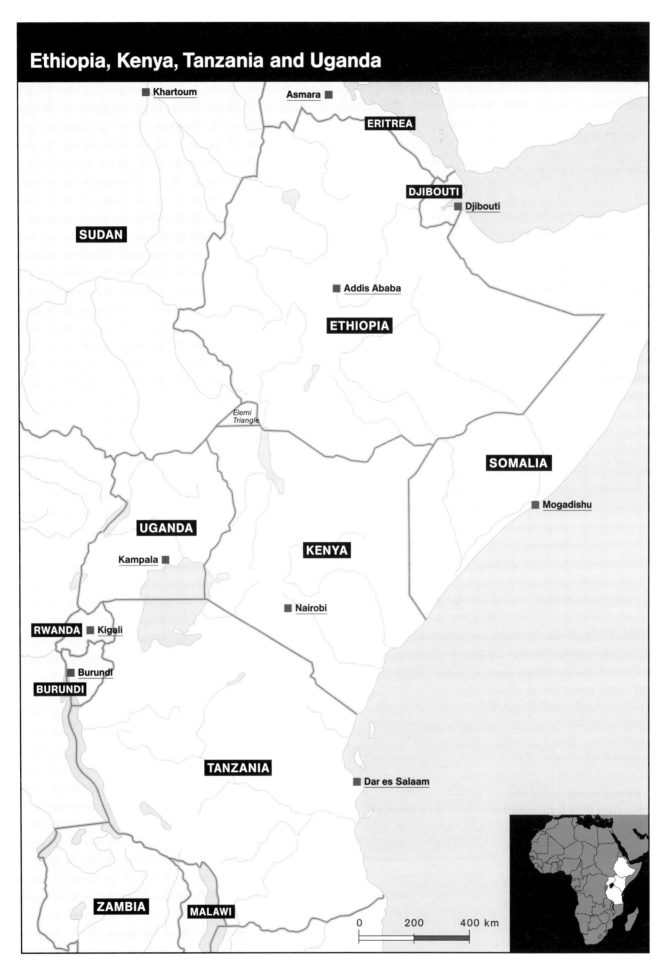

Khartoum

Asmara

ERITREA

DJIBOUTI

Djibouti

SUDAN

Addis Ababa

ETHIOPIA

Elemi
Triangle

SOMALIA

Mogadishu

UGANDA

Kampala

KENYA

Nairobi

RWANDA    Kigali

Burundi

BURUNDI

TANZANIA

Dar es Salaam

ZAMBIA    MALAWI

0    200    400 km

# Introduction

Colonization and commercialization have had a rapid and irreversible impact on pastoralist societies.[1] Agricultural expansion, environmental conservation, biofuel production, population pressure, climate change and conflict have all contributed to the increasing exclusion and vulnerability of pastoralists in eastern Africa and the Horn. But this process has not been experienced evenly throughout pastoralist society and it is often women who have suffered the greatest losses.[2]

Pastoralist women endure harmful customs such as female genital mutilation (FGM) and continue to have less access to public services in areas that already lag far behind the provisions available in other parts of their countries. Few options are available to control productive assets such as livestock and land, and women are often unable to inherit property. Women are also excluded – implicitly or explicitly – from community decision-making, which is firmly in the hands of male elders. However, although they are marginalized, these women not only run their homes and raise their children, but are also livestock managers, peacemakers and, on rare occasions, have managed to be elected into national and regional government.

Many lessons can be learned from those pastoralist women who have become leaders in their own communities. While they reveal individual determination and innovation, they also show that the structural causes of pastoralist women's marginalization have yet to be addressed. Although multi-party democracy has provided an arena for pastoralists to represent themselves in the political arena, as well as an opportunity to be consulted over the planning and implementation of development projects, pastoralist women are almost entirely absent from the decision-making process and the effectiveness of pastoralist parliamentarians in general is far from clear.[3]

As representation is limited, enduring perceptions of pastoralism continue to shape the view of governments throughout the region. Over-grazing, drought and desertification are believed to be the inevitable consequences of the pastoralist way of life and, for decades, livestock herders have been seen as a constraint to rural development. As a result, sedentarization has been consistently and continually promoted across the region, often against the will of pastoralist communities. In addition, development-induced displacement remains a common occurrence as pastoralists are relocated, sometimes by force, to make way for national interests.[4]

Pastoralism nonetheless remains one of the predominant livelihoods in eastern Africa and the Horn. Ethiopia has the largest pastoralist population in the region, found predominantly in the Afar and Somali Regions as well as in Borana Zone of Oromia Region and in South Omo Zone of the Southern Nations, Nationalities and People's Region. The majority of Kenya's pastoralists are found in the North Eastern, Eastern and Rift Valley Provinces bordering Ethiopia, Somalia, Sudan, Tanzania and Uganda. In Tanzania, pastoralists can be found across the north of the country and in particular Arusha Region, while in Uganda they are spread throughout much of the country with only the Karamoja Sub-Region considered as being distinctly pastoralist.

Government and non-government interventions among these communities must acknowledge and address gender imbalances, as changes that exclude women will quickly increase vulnerability, inequality and dependency. Pastoralist women are already more vulnerable than men and failing to understand how and why this is the case may well result in more harm than good. Working with pastoralist women to tackle the specific constraints on their participation will provide these women with the opportunity to attain greater power, prestige and ultimately representation in political office.

This report addresses the lack of pastoralist women's representation in Ethiopia, Kenya, Tanzania and Uganda. As pastoralists, they are victims of social, economic and political marginalization, and as women they suffer inequality in accessing resources, social services and participation in decision-making. In order to best address these issues, this report includes testimonies from pastoralist women who describe their own experiences as well as lessons learned from government officials and non-governmental interventions. To conclude, a series of recommendations aimed principally at policy-makers, non-government organizations (NGOs) and pastoralist women are listed at the end.

# Social exclusion

It is often stated that pastoralist men own and control livestock; dominate politics and decision-making; are the heads of households, lineages and clans; and see themselves as 'real' pastoralists. Women are left to play secondary, supportive roles in livestock production and hold subordinate roles to fathers, husbands and sons. They are excluded from public life while their identity as pastoralists is disparaged.[5] In some cases, this depiction is true. But it is important to keep in mind that it represents a gross simplification of pastoralist gender relations as well as the dynamism within pastoralist societies.

Prior to the commercialization of pastoralist products and resources, the incorporation of pastoralists into state systems, and the intervention of government and non-government development projects during the second half of the twentieth century, women appear to have held a more equitable position in their households and communities.[6] While this has been a far from uniform process, over the last century they have been marginalized and forced to relinquish any control they may have had over formal decision-making. Pastoralist women today are more vulnerable than they were in the past and are unable to directly voice their concerns to those who make decisions over their lives.

Women and girls tend to be regarded, and regard themselves, as the custodians of cultural values and beliefs, much more so than men and boys.[7] While some women regard this as a source of authority, since culture is not only defined but also imposed by men, women and girls become much more susceptible to gender discrimination. Their health and social status is adversely affected as well as their ability to participate fully in their communities.

Limited access to healthcare and education, high mortality rates, low life expectancies, and a lack of knowledge about family planning and reproductive health all indicate that pastoralist women continue to be disproportionately excluded from public services, which are already extremely limited. Although statistics are far from authoritative, as pastoralism has yet to be included on any national census and data is rarely disaggregated, they still reveal a consistent picture of women being marginalized from national resources and expenditure.

## Identity

As is widely recognized, custom and culture determine the social standing of men and women. Social norms enforced by male and female community elders continue to be observed irrespective of the growing body of legislation enacted to protect and promote women's rights. Among pastoralists in eastern Africa and the Horn, girls are socialized early on to accept their role as helpers to their mothers, who are themselves subordinate to their husbands. As the young girl grows older and enters marriage, she too will occupy the same position as her mother in a household that her husband heads. Folklore, stories, legends, sayings and proverbs help to reinforce these prescribed roles.[8] The impact this has on girls' education and their overall participation in society is described later in this report.

Girls are cast as the weaker sex and are taught to obey, respect and submit to the leadership of men. While young men gain prestige for trekking livestock to distant camps and protecting the community, young women are taught deference. Among the Maasai of Kenya and Tanzania, girls respond to greetings from men with shrill voices as a sign of deference to the caller. They continue to do this when they enter adulthood, as Clementina Meteyian, a Maasai woman from Tanzania, explains:

> 'Maasai women and girls are expected to have two voices, one for normal talk and another little voice used to demonstrate respect for men. Boys and men are not required to change their voices at any time.'[9]

However, the status of pastoralist women is also determined by numerous other factors, which can include age, class, religion and marriage status. In particular, there is ample evidence that demonstrates the exalted status of elderly, specifically widowed, pastoralist women in their own households and wider communities. An older Somali woman is respected and can take the lead in peacemaking if she is wise, speaks the truth and is concerned with the welfare of all people, irrespective of clan or other allegiance.[10]

The advent of colonialism and then independence tended to reinforce the status of men and undermined that of women. While Ethiopia was only occupied by Italy between 1936 and 1941, Kenya, Tanzania and Uganda all experienced lengthy periods of colonial rule that ended in the early 1960s. Although women appear to have contributed heavily to herd management throughout this time, they were not recognized as livestock owners and taxes were demanded from men based on the number of animals they held. When missionary and government schools began to be introduced in the first half of the twentieth century, it was boys who were the ones enrolled. Developments such as dairy cooperatives have also tended to assume that men own and control resources. Among the Maasai, this resulted in dairy herds being formally registered to male household heads, who in turn collected payment from collection points, irrespective of the fact that it was largely women who managed milk and milk products.[11] Women's diminishing control over livestock products such as milk has led to their growing vulnerability, a topic discussed in greater detail further on.

But more recently the declining importance of livestock in many pastoralist households and the increasing diversification of the pastoralist economy have both challenged the status of men. Emerging livelihoods such as small-scale trading, handicraft production and firewood collection have all been adopted by women, with men unwilling to engage in 'women's work'. In many cases the identity of pastoralist men is being undermined, as they cling to the remnants of livestock herds. As a result, pastoralist men are turning increasingly to alcohol as a distraction, which is often brewed and sold by pastoralist women.[12] In addition, among the Afar and Somali a growing problem is *khat*, a green leafy plant that acts as a mild narcotic.[13] As a result of *khat* consumption, women in Ethiopia's Somali Region shoulder an ever increasing burden to provide for themselves and their families.[14]

## Labour

Pastoralist production is entirely dependent on the complementary roles of men and women. Today, women's tasks may involve activities such as constructing houses, milking, managing sheep and goats, small-scale trading, producing butter, cheese and ghee, cultivating crops, producing handicrafts and collecting water, firewood, fodder, wild foods and non-timber forest products (NTFP). Until recently, men's roles have tended to remain much more restricted to livestock production and often include caring for and migrating with herds, managing grazing and water resources, collecting water, livestock trading, controlling predators, ensuring security, providing raiding parties, hunting and fishing, ploughing, collecting certain NTFPs and charcoal-making. However, in recent years men's labour has also shifted, with their growing involvement in non-pastoralist activities. As a result of out-migration to towns, many pastoralist men can now be found working as casual labourers, security guards and so on.

In Ethiopia, Kenya, Tanzania and Uganda, there are taboos in place that prohibit men from undertaking tasks deemed suitable only for women. This can often include collecting water and preparing food – tasks that a man would be ridiculed for undertaking. At the same time, while there are far fewer taboos limiting women's work,

there are examples of them being prohibited from milking livestock. The authority that women are able to exert over food as a result of these prohibitions allows them to influence the actions of their male kin. This is demonstrated later in this report with regard to the Samburu of northern Kenya, where women withhold food from even the most respected elders.

But, as a result, women work longer and harder than men and their workloads are rarely confined to the domestic environment as is often assumed. In addition, factors such as increased crop cultivation and environmental degradation are creating additional burdens for women. In support of this point, Denebo Dekeba, a Kerayu man from Central Ethiopia, estimates that 90 per cent of livestock activities are undertaken by women.[15] Bono Belanta, a Hamar woman from South Omo Zone, Ethiopia, who has founded her own women's association and competed in the 2005 elections, speaks for many:

> 'There is no limit to the work we do because all tasks wait for the woman ... I prepare breakfast then go to the field to farm, fetch water, take care of the children, build and repair the house, prepare food and take care of goats. Since there are no grinding mills we use our hands to grind flour. We do not get even a bit of rest.'[16]

However, while livestock represents a central element of pastoralism, agriculture is gaining greater importance for some pastoralist communities. For some this began many years ago while for others it has had little or no impact. Agro-pastoralism represents a partial settlement of the household and a dramatic shift in the division of labour. While men continue to herd livestock between distant satellite camps, women are left behind as the *de facto* household head responsible for all their previous tasks and have the added burden of crop cultivation.[17]

Female labour within the pastoralist economy is in such demand that girls are removed from school either temporarily or permanently, and women forgo many of the social occasions in which men make decisions and debate issues concerning the whole community. In light of this evidence, it is accurate to state that pastoralist households are dependent on the labour of women and girls who work from dawn to dusk, providing for their families' immediate needs, eking out additional incomes and tending livestock.

## Marriage

Pastoralist women pass between households and clans when they are married and are often not seen as permanent members of either. Marriage is an important part of pastoralist kinship relations and young women and men have little say in who they will marry. Early and forced marriages are common and bridewealth, as well as discriminatory inheritance, means that it is difficult to seek a divorce. Following the death of a husband, examples of wife inheritance can be found in certain pastoralist communities in all four countries. It is extremely difficult to nullify a union in many pastoralist societies, for example the Maasai, and this is especially true for women.[18]

Most marriages are arranged during adolescence or even earlier. Among the Maasai in Kenya and Tanzania, it is the women who choose potential partners, while among the Hor in South Omo Zone, Ethiopia, boys and girls first become acquainted and then decide mutually to get married. One reason for early marriage is the importance of bridewealth payments to the girl's family. The Hor, for example, exchange 30 to 40 goats and 20 to 30 kg of honey for the marriage. The recent introduction of guns and ammunition into bridewealth payments has also been observed along Uganda's border regions with Sudan and Kenya.[19]

With rising levels of poverty in pastoralist societies, women are increasingly becoming commoditized, as Juliana Auma from the Ethur community in Uganda illustrates:

*'The problem with paying bridewealth is that when a woman disagrees with a man over anything, the man reminds her that he paid a lot of animals for her. Also, since the whole clan contributes marriage animals, the whole clan controls women married to their clan. The woman's independence, self-esteem and dignity are reduced.'* [20]

Increasing bridewealth payments seem to have transformed the perception of women from mediators of social relations to pure commodities; the greater the 'value' one possesses the less freedom one has. For example, in one instance in 2006, a Member of Parliament for Karamoja, Uganda, gave 200 livestock as bridewealth in order to demonstrate his prestige.[21] Others, including Aneb Abdulkadir, a Member of Parliament from Ethiopia's Somali Region, assert that there is a deeper significance to bridewealth and that women are accorded greater respect than a simple commodity.[22]

Nevertheless, marriage arrangements involving bridewealth can be associated with rape and sometimes forceful abduction of girls, as is the case in Ethiopia's Afar Region.[23] It was only in 2001 that Ethiopia revised its Family Code to criminalize marriages that are not consensual, although in practice this has had little impact. In Karamoja, Uganda, the situation is the same, as Nakibus Lakara an elder from the Jie community explains:

*'You identify the girl, start wooing her, but sometimes it takes too long and so you decide to abduct and marry her. This usually happens while the girl is on her way to fetch water or firewood. Then you sleep with her forcefully. She goes to her home crying and that is when discussions about marriage start. In the meantime, ten lactating cows are being delivered to her family.'* [24]

However, while abduction is usually followed by marriage in Karamoja, should a man abduct a girl without the intention of marrying her, he would be perceived as a rapist and could even risk being killed. Violations are clearly criminalized but rape and abduction as part of the marriage 'process' is considered perfectly acceptable, as is evident from Nakibus Lakara's statement above. Unwanted marriages such as these have led some young women in Karamoja to commit suicide by drinking poison.[25]

A preference for cross-cousin marriage, known among the Afar, Somali and others, can also involve abduction. Afar girls may not even be informed when they are married to their *absuma*, or cousin, and are forcibly raped by their new husband. It is reported that this may occur over a period of many weeks, as most Afar girls are infibulated, which creates a physical barrier and makes sexual intercourse extremely painful for the women.[26]

As a man's herd accumulates, additional wives may be sought to form a polygamous household. A senior wife directs the labour of the junior wives, who are expected to provide the majority of the family's labour. These junior wives will shoulder the heaviest burden but are afforded even fewer rights than pastoralist women in general. As the husband is considered the household head, the family's resources are shared out between his co-wives. This can lead to conflict between the women, who try to secure the greatest portion for themselves and their children, and may even see the household temporarily break up during drought or other periods of crisis.[27]

Upon the death of the household head, his wife or wives will often be inherited by his brother or his cousin. This practice ensures that the children, as well as the property of the deceased, remain within the family or lineage. Although the new husband is expected to treat the widow and the children of his brother well, this is not always the case. Furthermore, some women may not wish to be inherited, which creates conflict between her and the family.[28]

However, among pastoralist societies where wife inheritance is not practised, a widow remains independent and is able to control her own destiny. Due to the age difference between spouses, there is often a high percentage of widows who head households. In many cases, a widow is often freer to do what she wants with her time and resources and can participate more fully in community life. But if she is without sons, she is likely to be among the poorest section of society.[29]

There is little evidence regarding the level of domestic violence between men and women in pastoralist households. In Afar Region, Ethiopia, physical abuse seems to be accepted as a necessary means of instilling discipline, although if serious harm is inflicted the marriage can be terminated. Yet this only happens in extreme cases, as wife battering is accorded little attention.[30] Sophia Abdi Noor, a Somali woman from northern Kenya who was nominated to the Kenyan Parliament, states:

> 'Wife battering is a way of men instilling discipline in their wives and daughters. It is not seen as a big issue even though evidence shows that it causes psychological and physical injuries to women … People simply say that she is just being disciplined a little, there is no problem.'[31]

But of course pastoralist women are not passive. Women's institutions have customarily mitigated the abuses of husbands and other male kin, such as the *ol-kishiroto* whereby Maasai women come together and mob a man, or a woman, who has violated sanctions.[32] Likewise, Boran women in northern Kenya and southern Ethiopia carry a stick called a *siiqqee*, which provides them with a symbolic rallying point for collective action. In extreme cases, a group of women will embark on a *godaansa siiqqee*, or *siiqqee* trek, abandoning their homes and children, leaving the men to look after them. Only by agreeing to pay a fine and performing a number of degrading and taboo actions can the perpetrator convince the women to return. If he continues his actions, he can be prohibited from holding any position of authority within the community.[33]

On a more subtle level, pastoralist women also assert themselves through the control of food production and distribution. The taboos that often prohibit men from these activities provide women with a means of authority over their husbands. Women can and do refuse to feed their husbands if they are unhappy with their behaviour.[34] As the providers of food, Samburu women from northern Kenya are empowered over even those elders who are generally seen to dominate society.[35] Likewise, Dassanetch women in South Omo Zone, Ethiopia, brew coffee for their husbands and will simply refuse to do so if they have been beaten or if they feel too much money has been spent on alcohol.[36]

These subtle strategies have often gone unnoticed by observers; nonetheless they represent important domains of power in the lives of pastoralist women. They highlight their determination to stand up for their rights and are, crucially, a clear resistance to submission. There is a very urgent need to understand the agency of pastoralist women; lack of research and planning can undermine what are already fragile rights. Understanding how and why women have lost much of the power and prestige that they appear to have controlled in the past is the first step to reinstating that authority.

## Education

Educational opportunities for pastoralists are dire, particularly for women and girls. Few attempts have been made to adapt educational services to pastoralist livelihoods and in some remote areas schools are still virtually unknown. Based on survey data of household respondents aged 6 and over, Table 1 shows the difference between the respective national averages of those who have never received any form of formal education, and the averages for some of the pastoralist areas.

In the pastoralist areas of Ethiopia, Kenya and Uganda there is a significantly lower chance of being educated than each of the national averages would suggest. Although the gender ratios remain high in the pastoralist areas, they are actually notably lower than each of the national averages. This suggests, although not conclusively, that the most important factor limiting pastoralist girls' education at present is not necessarily social or cultural

**Table 1:** No educational attainment, national average and pastoralist areas

| Country | Survey type & date | Region | Male (%) | Female (%) | Ratio |
|---------|--------------------|--------|----------|------------|-------|
| Ethiopia | DHS 2005 | National | 52.4 | 66.8 | 100:127 |
|  |  | Somali Region | 82.4 | 88.8 | 100:108 |
| Kenya | DHS 2003 | National | 15.8 | 22.9 | 100:145 |
|  |  | North Eastern Province | 65.8 | 86.8 | 100:132 |
| Tanzania | DHS 2004 | National | 24.7 | 33.3 | 100:135 |
|  |  | Arusha Region | 24.4 | 27.8 | 100:114 |
| Uganda | DHS 2006 | National | 12.3 | 23 | 100:187 |
|  |  | Karamoja Sub-Region | 52.7 | 66.5 | 100:126 |

barriers but rather a general lack of educational opportunities in the areas in which they live.

The situation in the Somali Region of Ethiopia is confirmed by a recent household survey that found that the literacy rate for male pastoralists was 22.7 per cent and for female pastoralists only 4.8 per cent, which suggests an even greater gender disparity than the data presented here.[37] Likewise, primary school gross enrolment rates compiled by the government of Kenya for 1998 indicate that the North Eastern Province has by far the lowest level of enrolment at only 32 per cent for boys and 16.8 per cent for girls.[38] It was also recently reported that the primary school enrolment rate in Karamoja was only 35 per cent, although no gender-disaggregated information is given.[39]

The data for Arusha Region in Tanzania appear anomalous, as educational attainment is comparable to the national average and girls are actually more likely to have received some education. This is most likely to have been caused by the heterogeneity of the region, which contains a major city that accounts for approximately 20 per cent of the population. More detailed data based on individual districts within Arusha Region that have higher pastoralist populations confirms a relatively high enrolment, which is again comparable to the national average, but identifies an extremely high gender ratio that suggests there are more than 25 per cent more boys than girls attending primary school.[40]

What these findings reveal, somewhat tentatively, is that while governments throughout eastern Africa and the Horn have recognized the gender gap in education, they have failed to address the limitations placed on pastoralists in general and pastoralist women in particular. While the steps taken to increase girls' education on a national level have significantly contributed to universal primary education, few such commitments have been made in pastoralist regions. In general, governments have attempted to adapt pastoralism to services rather than services to pastoralism.[41]

As a result, although it appears that pastoralists have an increasingly positive view of education, opportunities are few. In addition, there is less commitment towards girls' education than there is towards that of boys. As has been discussed, girls' labour is in greater demand and bridewealth results in early marriage and the abandonment of education. In Marsabit District, northern Kenya, the Boran also perceive few opportunities for pastoralist women to find paid employment that requires an education, which is a significant determining factor in this and many other instances.[42] There is also the fear of rape and sexual harassment as well as the belief that an educated girl will not accept marriage arrangements, jeopardizing her family's important bridewealth payments. Linah Jebii Kilimo, a pastoralist woman from Marakwet and Chair of the Kenya Women Parliamentary Association (KEWOPA), states bluntly:

> 'Parents lose interest in supporting somebody who will move away; why invest in someone who will leave you and who will be exchanged for property?'[43]

Equally critical is the widely held perception that education provides an escape from the pastoralist economy, or at the very least it will allow a child, most often a son, to access an urban income for the overall good of the household. It appears that few pastoralists value the thought of an educated man or woman continuing to practise pastoralism. This also reflects an important element of many pastoralists' views towards individual growth, which is rarely considered in the development and implementation of education services. Family prosperity rather than individual well-being is prioritized and can often be maximized by educating boys for as long as possible and keeping girls at home. In doing so, girls will become 'good' wives and gain their parents bridewealth, while boys will gain the skills to earn incomes both from pastoralism and, if need be, in the town.[44]

Alternatives to formal education are often seen as the way to address these issues, although there is the danger that they may result in a segregated system. Where alternatives have been attempted they have remained small-scale interventions with limited impact.

The Alternative Basic Education Programme for Karamoja (ABEK), which was established in 1998 by the government of Uganda and Save the Children, is one such example. According to Save the Children, by 2006, ABEK had established 268 learning centres, which had hosted 42,250 learners, 1,427 of whom had gone on to formal education. However, its impact has been limited due to a lack of technical capacity.[45] Girls in particular have not benefited since, once they reach early adolescence, they are often taken out of school to be married, a situation that has not changed significantly even after the introduction of food rations tied to attendance.[46] It is clear that a concerted effort will be needed to change attitudes to girls' education, as Paul Abul, District Education Officer for Moroto notes:

> 'In Karamoja, parents believe that if their daughters attain formal education they will become less competent wives, prostitutes or run off to marry non-Karimojong men who will divert them from the Karimojong ways of life.'[47]

Similar interventions have taken place elsewhere, with the appearance of boarding schools and mobile facilities, although few of these are integrated with national systems. This is partly due to the dismal prospects of pastoralist children being able to transfer into more formal schooling. Nonetheless, there has been some political will to support these measures. In Kenya, the Pastoralist Parliamentary Group successfully lobbied for an increased budget for boarding schools in pastoralist areas.[48]

As few attempts have been made to address the issues negatively affecting girls' school attendance, such as heavy workloads, early marriage and FGM, discussed below, these efforts have had little impact. Many girls grow up receiving no education at all due to other responsibilities, and those who are enrolled tend to drop out once they reach adolescence in order to undergo FGM and to get married. Although there are exceptional cases, attitudes towards girls' education remain negative.

In general, pastoralists are presented with scant evidence of the benefits of education, as there are few educated professionals among them who attain significantly higher standards of living than the rest of the community. Efforts are being made to change this perception, which are discussed later, but as MP in the Ugandan Parliament, Margaret Aleper Achila, Women's Representative for Kotido District in Karamoja, notes:

*'Those who have not gone to school are honourable leaders with authority and respect. Those educated are still answerable to them. So why educate? Who is to highlight the value of education?'*[49]

## Health

Mortality rates and life expectancies for pastoralists in eastern Africa and the Horn are generally considered unreliable due to lack of census data, illiteracy and under-reporting of deaths. With this in mind, Ethiopia's 1994 national census records the most surprising findings, indicating that women in the predominantly pastoralist Afar and Somali Regions actually have shorter life expectancies than men in those areas. The average life expectancy of a woman in Afar Region is only 47 while in Somali Region it is 53. This is

six years and three years less than men respectively and entirely contrary to both national and regional trends.

Patterns of inter- and intra-household discrimination identified among women and girls in Somali Region help to explain these discrepancies. From birth, boys are fed more and taken to a health clinic when they are sick, while girls are fed leftovers and treated with herbs. In fact, today there are twice as many men than women over the age of 60 in Ethiopia's Somali Region.[50]

Even more striking are the figures obtained from Karamoja Region in Uganda, which has by far the lowest average life expectancies in the country; only 44.9 for women and 39.7 for men in 2002.[51] This is generally explained as a result of conflict and associated hardship. Much more ambiguous is the available data on the Maasai in both Kenya and Tanzania. Sampling carried out concurrently in both countries identifies an extremely high average life expectancy for Maasai women, particularly in Tanzania where a figure of over 80 is recorded. This is partly explained by the difficulties of collecting data among the Maasai, who never refer to a dead person and in particular deaths related to childbirth, thus highlighting the limitations and unreliability of pastoralist data in general.[52]

Maternal mortality appears to be a major cause of death among pastoralist women. Among the Gabbra in northern Kenya, it was reported that there were 599 deaths per 100,000 live births in the mid-1990s; a far higher rate than the national rural average of 95.6.[53] Contemporary data from Karamoja Region in Uganda records an even higher figure of 750 deaths per 100,000 live births.[54] One factor influencing this is harmful traditional practices, such as withholding food from a pregnant woman during the final months of pregnancy in order to ease childbirth, which can be found among the Maasai in Kenya and Tanzania as well as some other pastoralist groups.[55] Table 2 shows that women in pastoralist areas are also far less likely to have any form of medical assistance than women in other parts of the country, which greatly increases the chance of maternal mortality.

**Table 2:** No antenatal care, national average and pastoralist areas

| Country | Survey type & date | Region | Percentage |
|---------|--------------------|--------|-----------|
| Ethiopia | DHS 2005 | National | 71.5 |
| | | Somali Region | 92 |
| Kenya | DHS 2003 | National | 9.6 |
| | | North Eastern Province | 68.3 |
| Tanzania | DHS 2004 | National | 3 |
| | | Arusha Region | 13.6 |
| Uganda | DHS 2006 | National | 4.5 |
| | | Karamoja Sub-Region | 6.4 |

**Table 3:** No childhood vaccinations, national average and pastoralist areas

| Country | Survey type & date | Region | Percentage |
|---------|-------------------|--------|------------|
| Ethiopia | DHS 2005 | National | 24 |
| | | Somali Region | 78 |
| Kenya | DHS 2003 | National | 7.4 |
| | | North Eastern Province | 45.7 |
| Tanzania | DHS 2004 | National | 4.3 |
| | | Arusha Region | 9.8 |
| Uganda | DHS 2006 | National | 6.6 |
| | | Karamoja Sub-Region | 2.2 |

Ethiopia appears to have particularly poor antenatal care throughout the whole country, while the greatest disparity can be observed in Kenya, where women in pastoralist areas are seven times more likely to give birth without antenatal care. The results for Arusha in Tanzania, although markedly lower than those for Ethiopia and Kenya, most likely the result of the same data deficiencies discussed above, nonetheless show that women are four times more likely to give birth without any assistance.

However, the most surprising result emerges from Karamoja Region in Uganda. Here, over 90 per cent of women reported receiving antenatal care, the vast majority of whom are served by a nurse or midwife. This level of medical service provision can also be observed in vaccination coverage of infants aged between 12 and 23 months, which is shown in Table 3, and indicates that nearly every infant in Karamoja has received some level of vaccination. These figures are difficult to explain, as Karamoja has extremely limited medical facilities. One possible factor may be the near constant presence of humanitarian organizations serving a large population of internally displaced people across northern Uganda, although this cannot be the only reason.[56]

HIV/AIDS also appears to be a significant problem for pastoralists, although authoritative data is unavailable. While little is known about its prevalence and transmission, factors such as culture, gender, poverty, conflict and displacement appear to be driving its spread.[57] Tables 4 and 5 indicate that married women from pastoralist areas are extremely unlikely to use contraceptives and that sexually active pastoralist women in general have comparatively less knowledge about the disease and its prevention than pastoralist men.

Misinformation about condoms is apparent in some instances and stems partly from the exclusion of pastoralists from health education.[58] For example, some Hamar elders in South Omo Zone, Ethiopia, believe that condoms actually cause AIDS because the two appeared at the same time.[59] Similarly, interviews with Maasai women in Tanzania reveal the widely held belief that condoms are ineffective and even dangerous, which helps to contextualize the data recorded for Arusha Region (Table 4):

*'I don't believe that they work – they're too thin and easy to break. Besides, what happens if they break inside the woman and cause her problems?'* [60]

**Table 4:** Married women not currently using any form of contraception, national average and pastoralist areas

| Country | Survey type & date | Region | Percentage |
|---------|-------------------|--------|------------|
| Ethiopia | DHS 2005 | National | 85.3 |
| | | Somali Region | 96.9 |
| Kenya | DHS 2003 | National | 60.7 |
| | | North Eastern Province | 99.8 |
| Tanzania | DHS 2004 | National | 73.6 |
| | | Arusha Region | 51.4 |
| Uganda | DHS 2006 | National | 76.3 |
| | | Karamoja Sub-Region | 99.4 |

**Table 5:** Knowledge that using condoms can prevent HIV (aged 15–49), national average and pastoralist areas

| Country | Survey type & date | Region | Male (%) | Female (%) | Ratio |
|---------|-------------------|--------|----------|------------|-------|
| Ethiopia | DHS 2005 | National | 64.3 | 40.2 | 100:63 |
| | | Somali Region | 15.8 | 10.6 | 100:67 |
| Kenya | DHS 2003 | National | 72 | 61 | 100:85 |
| | | North Eastern Province | 11.3 | 6.1 | 100:54 |
| Tanzania | DHS 2004 | National | 80.3 | 78.5 | 100:98 |
| | | Arusha Region | 75.6 | 66.6 | 100:88 |
| Uganda | DHS 2006 | National | 84.1 | 70 | 100:83 |
| | | Karamoja Sub-Region | 41.6 | 20.7 | 100:50 |

Subordinate social status and dependence on men to access resources such as livestock can often lead women to have a high risk of contracting HIV/AIDS. Pastoralist women may not be able to refuse unsafe sex, which helps to explain discrepancies in contraceptive usage. Furthermore, many non-Muslim pastoralist communities practise high-risk sexual behaviour.[61] For example, in Kenya and Tanzania, the Maasai see the exchange of semen as crucial for a girl's development, making the use of condoms extremely rare among the youth.[62] Partly as a result of this notion, early sexual debut is common. The prescribed sexual partners of *morans*, adolescent 'warriors', are pre-pubescent girls from the age of 10 or older. Although most girls actively participate in these encounters, if a girl reaches a certain level of physical maturity without having been initiated, she will be taken by force.[63]

Pastoralist men having sex with prostitutes and pastoralist women working as commercial sex workers – activities that were unheard of in the past – are also apparent. Schoolgirls who are boarding away from home, which is a necessity in many remote pastoralist areas, are thought to be particularly vulnerable, as is the case for the Hamar in Ethiopia among others.[64] Maasai women from both Kenya and Tanzania are known to work as prostitutes in the border town of Namanga, while pastoralist women across the region travel into local towns to work as prostitutes before returning to their communities.[65] There are also accounts of commercial sex between foreign tourists and both male and female pastoralists in Ethiopia and Kenya.[66]

However, research among the Maasai in Tanzania questions the widely held belief that HIV is simply transmitted to rural areas by return migrants. Here, it was found that Maasai men were not having sex while working in towns, as they had regulated their behaviour according to their perceptions of the disease. Even though they had obtained greater knowledge of HIV through exposure via television and other media, Maasai urban migrants nonetheless remain vulnerable, as condom use and understanding of HIV transmission continued to be limited.[67]

But arguably the single greatest factor in determining the health and social status of pastoralist women is FGM. Table 6 provides a comparison between the FGM prevalence rates in predominantly pastoralist areas and the respective national averages. In Ethiopia and Kenya women living in pastoralist areas have a nearly 100 per cent chance of undergoing FGM. In Tanzania, the figure

**Table 6:** Prevalence of female genital mutilation, national average and pastoralist areas

| Country | Survey type & date | Region | Percentage |
|---------|-------------------|--------|------------|
| Ethiopia | DHS 2005 | National | 74.3 |
| | | Somali Region | 97.3 |
| Kenya | DHS 2003 | National | 32.2 |
| | | North Eastern Province | 98.8 |
| Tanzania | DHS 2004 | National | 14.6 |
| | | Arusha Region | 54.5 |
| Uganda | DHS 2006 | National | 0.6 |
| | | Karamoja Sub-Region | 1.8 |

is lower but remains three times the national average, while in Uganda an extremely low prevalence is recorded.

FGM in itself is believed to contribute to the spread of HIV. Recent evidence from Kenya and Tanzania suggests that unhygienic practices associated with FGM, as well as male circumcision, may result in HIV transmission.[68] Whether this is substantiated or not, with no medical benefits or religious sanctioning, FGM remains a severe violation of women's rights and is a significant factor in their marginalization, which Linah Jebii Kilimo and many like her believe is abhorrent:

*'Pastoralists marginalize themselves further through FGM; this is where I feel the culture is a monster to the girl child.'*[69]

For pastoralists in eastern Africa and the Horn, FGM serves as a rite of passage, through which a girl becomes a woman. To participate fully in society, a girl is forced to undergo the procedure. In Uganda, the Sabiny are one of the few groups that continue to practise FGM, based upon the belief that it is necessary to demonstrate maturity. Everlyn Chemtai chose to flee her Sabiny community to relatives in Kenya rather than to undergo FGM. However, when she returned to announce her political ambitions she was told not to waste her time, as she was still a 'child'.[70]

Despite interventions from the Family Planning Association of Uganda (FPAU) to eradicate the practice among the Sabiny by 2006, it is still in existence today. Girls who had previously been spared in adolescence are being forcefully mutilated upon marriage. Patrick Kitiyo, a councillor for FPAU, states that those who have not undergone the procedure:

*'…are referred to as "girls" and elders look at them as people who have nothing developmental to contribute to any debate and because society has also deemed it a taboo for them to climb into granaries or even collect cow dung, these women have been forced to undertake circumcision to avoid harassment.'*[71]

In Kenya, Peris Tobiko, a Maasai woman, had a similar experience to Everlyn Chemtai when she announced her interest in the parliamentary seat for Kajiado District. When she started campaigning in her prospective constituency, she learned that there were whispers enquiring: *'Is she even circumcised, because if she is not, she cannot get votes.'*[72] She felt that her largely conservative Maasai constituents would not accept her legitimacy in Parliament and so did not vote for her.

Although girls often undergo FGM when they reach early adolescence, preparing them for marriage, this is not always the case. In many predominantly Muslim communities, girls experience FGM at a much younger age but do not get married until they are older. According to Sophia Abdi Noor:

*'FGM is a double-edged sword. They think it is in the Qur'an so they have to do it so that they do not violate religious teachings. Second, it is used to make a woman believe that she stands a better chance of getting married.'*[73]

FGM marginalizes those girls who undergo the procedure as few return to school and it alienates those girls who are spared, as they become outcasts with few opportunities to get married. Although some girls are able to return to school and become eligible for community involvement, the physical and psychological impacts cannot be taken lightly.

But despite the extent of FGM among pastoralists, it is extremely difficult to campaign against it at the national level. Linah Jebii Kilimo has spent much of her political life tackling the problem but has received scant recognition, and often derision, from her peers in the Kenyan Parliament.[74] In Uganda this problem is compounded as only a small minority still practise FGM and few parliamentarians see its significance in their own constituencies, as Winifred Masiko, Chair of the Uganda Women Parliamentary Association (UWOPA) explains:

*'We used to have a minister who came from that area [Sabiny] and she talked against FGM and wasn't voted back, which was an indication that it is not an issue that is appreciated yet; anyone who raises it will not be voted for.'*[75]

It is therefore imperative to expand as well as adapt public services for pastoralists. The failure to do so will reinforce their marginalization and increase their vulnerability to factors such as HIV/AIDS, as well as contributing to the continuation of FGM. At present, pastoralists have fewer schools and medical facilities than the rest, which is affecting their ability to participate in the national decision-making processes. Alternative or non-formal education would allow more pastoralist children to attend schools because households would not be forced to choose between vital labour inputs needed from their children for pastoralist production and sending a child to school. This is particularly important for girls who at present are forced to remain behind in favour of their brothers. Providing lessons that contribute to the pastoralist economy, for example veterinary skills, may also be perceived by families as an incentive to send more children to school.

# Economic exclusion

Without sufficient social capital, pastoralist women find it difficult to build an independent economic status. Although ownership and access to livestock is complex, women are generally unable to benefit from the principal output from the pastoralist economy, despite playing varied and often unacknowledged roles in livestock production. The commercialization of livestock products, land and NTFPs has also occurred at the expense of women, who have been marginalized from the domains of power they were previously associated with. Male inheritance remains the norm despite national legislation enforcing equitable inheritance of property.

In addition, conflict and environmental degradation have eroded the pastoralist economy and, because of the existing marginal status of women, they have also increased the vulnerability of women disproportionately to that of men. Female headed households have become entirely dependent on activities such as firewood and grass collection in order to eke out subsistence living standards. With few assets or savings, and with little or no access to financial services, these households succumb more quickly to crises and take longer to recover economically. For those who have lost their entire livestock herd, abandoning the pastoralist economy is often the only option and they are forced to settle on the outskirts of urban areas.

## Livestock

When it comes to describing pastoralist gender relations, many assert that women are unable to own and dispose of livestock, which represents not only the principal economic output of the pastoralist economy but also serves as a sign of prestige and social status. But a man often needs his wife or mother to access particular livestock, and the ownership of and access rights to a household's herd are complex and poorly understood in many cases.[76] However, women tend to have far greater rights to access and dispose of livestock products like milk, butter, cheese, ghee, hides and skins than they do over livestock itself.

For example, a Hamar widow can assert authority over her deceased husband's younger brother in instances when both his parents are also deceased, as she can assume a great deal of control over their livestock.[77] However, Hamar women have no power to sell livestock; they can only trade chickens, eggs, milk, hides and skins. They are not even allowed to sell agricultural produce that they have grown without first consulting their husbands.[78] The

same situation exists in Tanzania, as Paulina Tipap, a Maasai woman, explains:

> 'Women own no livestock and the value of their work is not appreciated. Even to sell a cow, permission has to be sought … in fact even to sell an ear of maize that I have planted myself, I have to do it secretly.'[79]

This is despite the central role that women have in livestock production, which is often overlooked. A great deal of their time is spent tending animals such as goats and sheep around the homestead. They also collect water and fodder for sick animals and have extensive knowledge concerning animal health.[80] In many cases, girls accompany boys and men when they trek livestock in order to cook and clean for them.

But while it appears that pastoralist women have rarely been able to dispose of livestock independently of their male kin, what is troubling is their loss of control over livestock products. Women have by custom maintained full authority over the production, distribution and disposal of livestock products, which has represented one of their few economic outlets. But a combination of commercialization and greater sedentarization, often associated with the adoption of agro-pastoralism or as a result of government policy, has begun removing women's control over milk, butter, cheese and ghee.[81]

Commercialization, whether for meat or milk production, tends to be realized by men. Women are unable to be engaged in this process because of their heavy workloads and lack of mobility. Men also have authority over the location of the household, which determines the accessibility of markets. Since livestock can be trekked to markets but livestock products cannot, men can establish full control over the commercial activities of all household members.[82] As a result, among the settled Maasai in Tanzania, men have taken over nearly all the activities previously associated with dairying by women, which has been aided by the tendency of development interventions to recognize men as herd owners, as evidenced above.[83]

In the search for alternatives to the dwindling authority of pastoralist women over livestock products, and in order to strengthen their livelihoods in general, many NGOs have assisted them to form savings and credit groups as well as legally recognized cooperatives. These provide opportunities to women who have few assets and who would otherwise have been unable to access credit from formal financial institutions, even if such institutions were present in pastoralist regions. As a result, many women have established individual or group businesses that purchase, process and trade in pastoralist products like livestock and milk, as well as other ventures including vegetables and handicrafts.[84]

However, while the interest of NGOs over the last decade has been to strengthen and support the pastoralist economy, the prevailing view among governments in the region is that pastoralism represents an archaic production system that needs to be changed. A large part of this is driven by the national focus on economic growth and the perception that the pastoralist economy is inefficient and a waste of vast tracts of 'no-man's land'. As a result, non-government interventions that target specific aspects of pastoralism, such as veterinary services, may be undermined in the long term by government agendas. One way of redressing this situation is an approach that seeks to identify the total economic value (TEV) of pastoralism. This framework takes into account both direct economic gains and indirect benefits such as biodiversity conservation and tourism.[85]

TEV studies for pastoralist systems in eastern Africa and the Horn have already been attempted, revealing significant contributions to gross domestic product (GDP) as well as numerous indirect benefits.[86] These studies should now be consolidated and used as the basis for innovative advocacy tools targeting government policymakers. However, greater effort needs to be made to disaggregate the available data, in order to highlight the different roles that pastoralist women and men play. This could help to promote government and non-government interventions that address the specific issues facing pastoralist women.

## Land

The consistent undervaluing of the pastoralist economy has led governments to allocate pastoralist rangelands for alternative uses and promote private land-holding in an attempt to increase productivity. Customarily, rangelands, forests and water resources were held as communal property, with access and use rights determined by group affiliation. Pastoralist women, for example Boran women from southern Ethiopia, were excluded from customary management regimes and relied on men to access natural resources.[87] But the loss of dry season rangelands and access to permanent water sources has drastically altered these systems by reducing pastoralist mobility and increasing sedentarization, which has differing impacts on pastoralist women and men.

Although colonial authorities began the alienation of pastoral resources, the process was actually intensified

after independence.[88] Pastoralists are not recognized as the owners of their own lands, which are inevitably declared as belonging to the state. Agricultural biases on the part of planners have in turn promoted the expansion of settled crop cultivation in pastoralist regions, despite its incompatibility with arid and semi-arid lands. In Tanzania, the Barabaig claim they have suffered continual encroachment onto their grazing land by Iraqw agro-pastoralists, who they believe are being encouraged and supported by the state. As James Getaru somberly states:

> 'There is no law to prevent Iraqw from taking all our land because the government system does not permit our participation.'[89]

This small-scale agricultural expansion has also occurred alongside large-scale, irrigated, state-sponsored mechanized plantations. One area where this has been experienced most intensively is the Lower Awash Valley, Ethiopia, where Afar and Kerayu pastoralists have had their customary access rights revoked in favour of cotton and sugarcane plantations and a national park.[90]

Because of the stewardship of pastoralist producers, many arid and semi-arid rangelands have also retained a rich biodiversity of flora and fauna. This has encouraged the establishment of national parks, wildlife sanctuaries and controlled hunting zones in what are often dry season grazing lands that are crucial for pastoralists. Gazetting and the criminalization of pastoralist livelihood activities such as livestock herding, hunting and fishing is the standard response from governments and many conservation agencies. In September 2007 the Basongora of Uganda became one of the latest pastoralist communities to be evicted from a designated conservation area, when 8,000 people were removed from Queen Elizabeth National Park.[91] Prior to the eviction, Amos Isimbwa of the Basongora community expressed his hopes:

> 'We want the government to correct the injustices of the colonial times committed against us. We want the land that was taken away from us after independence. We should also be given an avenue through which we can exercise our rights and all those persecuting us too should be charged under the law.'[92]

Most recently the rangelands of eastern Africa and the Horn have been annexed from their customary users so that biofuels can be produced. In Ethiopia, 60,000 hectares of dry season grazing land on the banks of the Omo River in South Omo Zone were leased to an Italian firm for a period of 70 years in order to grow palms and jatropa. Although plans have been put in place to provide 1 per cent of the output to the region, there seems to have been little attempt to offset the losses faced by Hamar and Dassanetch agro-pastoralists among others.[93] In Kenya, a plan to produce biofuels in the Tana Delta was approved by the government in June 2008, but it has been heavily criticized due to concerns over both biodiversity and livelihoods. The delta provides crucial grazing land for up to 60,000 livestock during the dry season.[94]

Although resource losses are endured collectively, women are often less able to negotiate with private or group land-holding systems, which are emerging among pastoralists as a response to increasingly insecure tenure. For example, the Samburu were initially encouraged to form group ranches by the government of Kenya, and membership was granted exclusively to male household heads. The subsequent establishment of individual land-holdings has continued this trend, although a small number of women have been granted land by the District Land Adjudication Officer, despite opposition from the local land committee.[95]

In Tanzania, Maasai and Parakuyo pastoralists were evicted from the Mkomazi Game Reserve in the late 1980s. Impoverishment increased most households' reliance on women's income, derived from milk, chickens, medicinal plants and animal hides. Workloads among the Maasai and Parakuyo women duly increased, although sedentarization did result in women gaining greater authority over their own earnings as well as greater access to educational and health facilities.[96] Sedentarized Ariaal and Rendille women in northern Kenya have likewise retained their customary control over milk and crops, resulting in significant social gains from market demand and a corresponding increase in economic autonomy.[97]

Effectively, sedentarization in these latter cases has acted to empower pastoralist women economically through market integration, which has in turn advanced their social status. However, while the status of pastoralist women has been improved in some instances, sedentarization very often results in acute poverty and severe environmental degradation. While the impact on women should not be overlooked, the long-term social, economic and environmental consequences of more sedentary lifestyles far outweigh the gains. These same gains can be made in a more appropriate way only when pastoralists are included in development planning. More inclusive development will serve to protect lifestyles and livelihoods that are tailored to the environment while at the same time not denying pastoralists the benefits of national development.

## Environment

Natural resources in the pastoralist areas of eastern Africa and the Horn are suffering from environmental degradation brought about by climate change, over-exploitation

and the decline of customary management regimes. As a great many of the tasks performed by women are closely involved with the exploitation of natural resources, their workloads have also increased rapidly. For example, as a consequence of increased migration in search of water and pasture, houses must be dismantled, transported and rebuilt with greater frequency.[98]

In Ethiopia and Kenya, a significant change has been the appearance of invasive species including *Prosopis Juliflora* (mesquite), a small thorny tree or shrub native to the Americas, on the rangelands. As well as stifling native species, *Prosopis* can pose a danger to livestock and is generally considered as one of the greatest threats to the pastoralist economy.[99] Due to the use of chemical fertilizers and pesticides, commercial agricultural has also degraded fertile rangelands and water sources. Kajiado and Nakuru Districts in Kenya and Simanjiro District in Tanzania have suffered serious cases of water pollution due to the contamination from flower farms upstream.[100] In South Omo Zone, Ethiopia, the pesticides used on a private cotton plantation have wiped out the entire bee colony of the neighboring Tsamako agro-pastoralists, leaving one man stating that:

*'They should either leave our country or kill us all and cultivate our land.'*[101]

The depletion of forest resources increases the time needed to collect firewood and many impoverished female heads of households are now entirely dependent on the resource and exploit it more intensively. Materials for house construction such as thatching grass and wood are also coming under threat. Among the Samburu in northern Kenya, men have begun constructing modern houses, and as a result end up using more wood, which increases the burden on women whose role it is to collect and carry the materials.[102]

It is also important to consider that NTFPs such as medicinal plants, fruits, nuts, honey, beeswax and gum resins are increasingly becoming significant contributors to household incomes and are important for subsistence.[103] Handicraft production in particular is becoming an important livelihood strategy for some pastoralist women and has grown with the spread of tourism, although it remains a notoriously fickle market. Handicrafts generally use communally held natural resources, although access and use rights can change to the detriment of women as commercialization and exploitation intensifies. Turkana women in northern Kenya also harvest and process aloe for commercial sale within the district, which they hope to expand to neighbouring communities.[104]

Women's knowledge of the environment is particularly crucial during times of drought, as livestock mobility is increased and women are almost always the ones left behind to manage the household. Of course, richer pastoralist households can withstand the impacts of drought for longer, but poorer pastoralists, a category that often includes female headed households, are less resistant to shocks. But despite the roles that women play in drought mitigation and the particular vulnerabilities they face, state-led drought mitigation measures do not include the views of women:

> '... drought policies are designed only by men: these policies are silent about the vulnerabilities of women to climatic hazards. Ignoring the realities and needs of half of their societies undermines ... the viability and effectiveness of any drought response.'[105]

An important coping strategy adopted by pastoralist women is the collection of wild foods to supplement their families' diets, although their availability is continually being reduced because of environmental degradation and land privatization.[106] Women also distribute livestock products among themselves throughout the year, so that they may support each others' households in times of heightened vulnerability. These informal groups may also engage in small-scale trading during times of drought.[107] Among the Boran in northern Kenya, richer households or those that have not been affected so seriously from drought transfer milk cows to those left destitute, although the frequency and severity of drought threatens to undermine the system.[108]

There is a pressing need for policy-makers to begin to see pastoralism as the solution to environmental degradation, not the cause. Recognizing the significance of pastoralist production methods in conserving the current biodiversity of arid and semi-arid rangelands would be a significant step in the right direction. Criminalizing pastoralist livelihoods and evicting pastoralists from areas deemed important for wildlife conservation will endanger both the local economy and conservation efforts. In many cases, customary rangeland management regimes have been undermined due to the intervention of the state and need to be reinstated.

Pastoralist women should be identified as having key roles to play in conservation as they are most likely to manage and, increasingly, depend on these resources for their livelihoods. With natural resources becoming increasingly important for household well-being, particularly for those households headed by women, value chains for the marketing of particular natural resources both locally and nationally are needed. This should include assessing the feasibility of processing environmental resources around the home, which is crucial to avoid marginalizing pastoralist women during commercialization.

## Conflict

Women have an ambiguous role in pastoralist conflicts. They are not only victims but also catalysts of violence. On the one hand, they may encourage or even provoke their male kin to become involved in acts of violence by cultivating a notion of hero worship. In some cases, even the wife of a successful fighter is accorded greater respect.[109] Women may also demand high bridewealth payments from the men they have been betrothed to and then ridicule them until they have secured it through raiding.[110] On the other hand, as women are non-combatants and tend to have less restrictive ties to given clans or lineages, they often lead the way in making peace. But whatever their role may be, women nearly always suffer the greatest hardships during conflict. In Karamoja they are targeted as the mothers of future generations of 'enemies' and, as retribution, they are victims of abduction, rape and murder.[111] Furthermore, when casualties occur, the burden falls on women to support the household; a difficult task as the household may have already been impoverished by livestock raids.[112]

> 'We women live with permanent worry. We don't know if we will live to see the next day. We can't gather wild fruits – before you can even hit the tree to knock them down, you fear someone will hear you. If we are captured we are harassed or attacked. We lose our children – even if we survive ourselves, we are never the same. When a child dies, part of your self has gone. We may die ourselves in raids. We lose livestock, our means of survival, so poverty kills us slowly.'[113]

As well as livestock raiding, particularly fuelled by the need to secure bridewealth payments during a time of increasing poverty, concerns over land and natural resources have been major factors in increased conflict in eastern Africa and the Horn. However, conflicts in pastoralist areas are inevitably much more complex, involving regional, national and even international forces. The legacy of colonial state formation often complicates both the disputes and the attempts at resolution, as cooperation between neighbouring states has proven to be particularly challenging. While environmental degradation and climatic shocks such as droughts contribute to this violence, they are never the sole cause of conflict.

Disarmament has not been easy. In Karamoja, Uganda, there has been a near constant supply of weapons for many years partly due to the lack of coordination between neighbouring countries with regard to disarmament.[114] In addition to the more obvious consequences, domestic violence involving weapons has increased dramatically among the Karamojong.[115] In general, the proliferation of small arms has served to empower men as combatants and as owners of weapons, as Oscar Oketch explains:

*'There are warlords, men in their 40s. They are wealthy and they control all arms. They conduct organized raids and they are brave. They come back with thousands of animals and they have a say in who is to be elected. Since warlords are men, women have no room.'* [116]

Nonetheless, women have come together on a number of occasions to challenge these forces and attempt to build a lasting peace. Somali women throughout the region are renowned as skilled and effective brokers and mediators between factions, which they can achieve through their marriage ties between clans.[117] In Kenya's northern Wajir Province, women began a dialogue for peace that brought clan leaders face to face. Their efforts resulted in the Wajir Peace and Development Committee (WPDC) comprised of Members of Parliament, religious leaders, NGOs, the security forces as well as women and elders.[118] Dekha

Ibrahim Abdi, who co-founded WPDC, is now a prominent pastoralist women peace-builder, a trustee on a number of peace-building associations and a widely published author. In 2007, she was awarded the Right Livelihood Award for her efforts to bring about peace in northern Kenya.

However, the respect accorded to particularly skilled women negotiators like Dekha Ibrahim Abdi does not translate into support for pastoralist women seeking political office. Men, considered the perpetrators of violence, rather than women, perceived as the bringers of peace, are still seen as the natural candidates when it comes to the ballot box. Allyce Kureyia, a Rendille woman from northern Kenya, unsuccessfully campaigned for office in 2007 but remains optimistic, as she sees that Members of Parliament do not have to take up arms to resolve a situation:

*'Following past banditry incidents, the Member of Parliament did not take up arms to fight bandits. But he spoke against it in Parliament. I can do that much better.'* [119]

# Political exclusion

Pastoralist women in eastern Africa and the Horn have struggled to compete with men in the political arena, and only a few have succeeded in campaigning for an open parliamentary seat. Affirmative action and reservations mean that both Tanzania and Uganda can boast a 30 per cent representation of women in Parliament. But in both cases, the actual number of women directly elected by constituents is far smaller. In Tanzania it is only 5 per cent and conversely, in Ethiopia and Kenya, where no system of reservations has been adopted, overall representation stands at 22 per cent and only 9 per cent respectively.[120]

Despite the great disparity in Kenya, resistance towards a quota for women was intense in the months before the disputed December 2007 elections. A campaign for 50 special seats for women was spearheaded by KEWOPA but their efforts were ignored when the house failed to form the required quorum for a constitutional amendment.[121] Women were eventually elected for 15 seats, but the greatest success was the appointment of seven women in an enlarged cabinet of 42. However, the Kenyan Parliament subsequently failed to elect a single woman onto any of the key House Committees; currently their greatest representation is in the Catering Committee.[122]

## Elections

It is extremely difficult to identify who is a pastoralist in the political processes of Ethiopia, Kenya, Tanzania and Uganda because prospective and existing Members of Parliament are not profiled in such a way. In addition, some who come from a pastoralist background choose to distance themselves from their constituents upon election. However, although pastoralist women are under-represented it is possible to identify some who have been able to gain political office in each of the four countries.

In Uganda, Florence Adong Omwony successfully campaigned for Labwor County, Abim District, and is the only women parliamentarian to be elected from Karamoja Region, but is not considered a pastoralist.[123] As Winifred Masiko explains:

*'In other areas, women have been competing for the general seats, where men usually compete, but in Karamoja this hasn't happened; in most of the pastoralist areas, the women are still highly marginalized.'*[124]

Uganda also guarantees women a seat from every District, which means that each District in Karamoja has a female representative.[125] However, while guarantees are made for women there is no provision for minority status, so women from communities such as the Karamojong or Jie do not necessarily hold these seats. A petition was submitted in June 2008 for such provisions but an outcome has yet to be announced.[126] In addition, the authority of District Women Representatives is limited, as they do not build support through campaigning and must represent multiple constituencies with the same financial resources as elected Members of Parliament.[127]

The only elected pastoralist woman in the Tanzanian Parliament appears to be Dr Mary Nagu, who is a Member of Parliament for the predominantly Barabaig constituency of Hanang and also serves as Minister of Industry, Trade and Marketing. Individual political parties also make reservations for women based on the overall number of seats they hold in the Parliament. But again it is important to note that some, including the current Deputy Speaker of the National Assembly Anna Makinda, believe that those who do not campaign for seats are forming a 'second tier', with less legitimacy and lobbying capacity than their elected counterparts.[128]

On a positive note, in Kenya there are now two elected and two nominated pastoralist women in the Parliament despite the apparent exclusiveness of the Kenyan political system noted above. Linah Jebii Kilimo was re-elected for a second term as Member of Parliament for Marakwet East, Rift Valley Province, on a Kenya National Democratic Alliance (KENDA) ticket and is also serving as Assistant Minister for Cooperative Development. In an unexpected result, Hellen Sambili became the first women representative of Mogotio, Rift Valley Province, on a United Democratic Movement (UDM) ticket and was also appointed Minister for Youth and Sports. The former Egerton University professor overcame an experienced field of five men to be narrowly elected by the mainly Kalenjin-Tugen community.[129] Sophia Abdi Noor, a Somali from North Eastern Province, was nominated by her Orange Democratic Movement (ODM) party and is now serving on the Health, Housing, Labour and Social Welfare Committee. Likewise, Maison Leshoomo, a Samburu from Rift Valley Province and a district chair of the Maendeleo ya Wanawake Organization, was nominated by the Party of National Unity (PNU) and is now serving on the Fiscal Analysis and Appropriation Committee.[130]

But the greatest number of elected pastoralist women parliamentarians can be found in Ethiopia. Neima Ahmed Yusuf, one of three women in the Pastoral Affairs Standing Committee, was elected by her constituents in Miaso, Oromia Region, at the age of only 23. In Somali Region, Aneb Abdulkadir was elected in Aware and is also a member of the Foreign, Defence and Security Affairs Standing Committee. Fatuma Abdela Alimirah was elected in Gewane and is the only women parliamentarian from Afar Region, while also serving as a member of the Capacity Building Affairs Standing Committee. Finally, Nakia Ankosiya Aymela was elected by her Dassanetch constituents in South Omo Zone. With the exception of Aneb Abdulkadir, who was married to Ethiopia's Permanent Representative to the United Nations, the late Dr Abdul Mejid Hussein, all are very junior Members of Parliament with limited experience. In Somali Region two women were also integrated into the *gurti*, or Council of Elders, although it seems they have been unable to influence decisions:

*'We only listen, and try not to interfere with the proceedings of the elders on the Gurti committee.'*[131]

It is important to take note that the two countries that operate extensive affirmative action for women – Tanzania and Uganda – actually have the smallest number of pastoralist women parliamentarians directly elected by constituents, which suggests that the system has not favoured women from minority groups. A great deal of concern is also expressed over the legitimacy of those women who have been nominated as Members of Parliament. Party quotas may offer greater opportunities for those women who have remained marginalized, although much would remain to be done. Supporting those pastoralist women who have become leaders and facilitating the involvement of others is therefore crucial. The few women who have risen to the top need greater support from both specially mandated pastoralist parliamentary groups and from women's parliamentary associations. Role models from the community also need to be supported by NGOs.

## Attitudes

Confrontations between state authorities and pastoralists in eastern Africa and the Horn continue to be troubled. Many pastoralist communities, particularly those that are numerically small, have never had any political representation at the parliamentary level. This has bred a culture of avoidance and rejection among pastoralist communities with regard to the state. Maria Endagaw, a Barabaig woman from Hanang District in Tanzania, puts it bluntly:

*'We despise governmental things so we avoid them.'*[132]

As a result, concerns over women's participation will often be overshadowed by concerns over political representation in general. Beyond this view, negative attitudes regarding the role of pastoralist women continue to represent a significant barrier to female participation. Women themselves consistently campaign and vote in large numbers to elect male candidates into political positions, even on the occasions when a woman candidate is competing. When Mumina Konso, a Boran woman from Isiolo District in northern Kenya, made her interest in politics public, she was told by many other women to run for the position of councillor, since they perceived the role of a Member of Parliament as being too big for a woman to manage.[133]

For the same reasons, women also continue to perform and condone FGM, which leads to a vicious circle when it comes to politics. As Everlyn Chemtai and Peris Tobiko explained, girls often do not return to school once they undergo FGM, while those who are spared are regarded as children. The dilemma is difficult, but it is one that Linah Jebii Kilimo was able to exploit in order to be elected twice as Member of Parliament for Marakwet East in northern Kenya:

*'I ran away from home. I don't know where I was running but I was running away from the knife, because I was scared that after being circumcised it means getting married and stopping education … Today, I accept the fact that I am a child according to their perceptions. But I tell them that to be a leader – to be a Member of Parliament – is to be a servant. And whom do you send to be a servant? You don't send a grown up, you send a child.'*[134]

But even if a woman can win the confidence and support of her own community, she must then face the challenges of the political process. The unsavoury language and harsh campaigning schedules make many pastoralist men and women wary of competing, particularly against established male incumbents.[135] In Kenya, Tiyah Galgalo's campaign for a parliamentary seat led to criticism over her divorce and failure to remarry, and she was even branded a prostitute.[136] Male politicians will even resort to using their constituencies' patriarchal culture to undermine women. In Kenya, Peris Tobiko was able to secure the nomination from the Orange Democratic Movement Party of Kenya (ODM-K) for Kajiado Central. However, the incumbent scolded her clan for using a woman to compete against him, and added:

*'Please advise your friend to go and seek votes from the district where she is married. She was given away. What is she still doing where she was born?'*[137]

Likewise in Uganda, UWOPA loses many female candidates soon after they face the reality of political life. Even when a woman is successful, she often chooses not to compete for a second term, as the rigors of holding political office and running a household become too overwhelming.[138] With such high turnover in political office across the region in general, and the difficulties facing women in particular, capacity-building remains limited and the effectiveness of pastoralist women parliamentarians is undermined.

## Capital

Pastoralist women face many barriers to accessing and controlling both social and financial capital, as evidenced earlier in this report. Socially, women are not leaders in their own communities. Financially, women are excluded from accessing and disposing of livestock and have very few inheritance rights, as Winifred Masiko outlines:

> *'Economic empowerment still disfavours women and that reduces greatly their powers to compete in politics, and of course we still have cultural issues where people think politics is a no-go area for women.'*[139]

To build the social and economic capital required for political participation, a woman is forced to be dependent on her husband and other male relatives. Through them, she may access the social networks of her household and clan as well as finances that are most often held as livestock. But in many cases it is unlikely as her male kin expect that she work within the household. As Ndinini Kimesera Sikar, of the Maasai Women Development Organization (MWEDO) in Tanzania, explains:

> *'We are in a patriarchal system where men have power and women do not. Within this system, for a woman to venture into politics she needs the go-ahead from her husband, she needs his blessings, she needs his support and that of his friends and relatives, without it, a woman cannot make it.'*[140]

The dependency on men is justified through myths that perpetuate the respective statuses of women and men.[141] As a result, established male incumbents are unlikely to be challenged, as they are supported by networks of allegiances among and often between clans. In Kenya, Sophia Abdi Noor's first campaign in 1997 ended when she was disqualified due to her opponent's authority:

> *'The incumbent was a powerful politician who was once also an ambassador and had easy access to the President. He went and told the President that*

> *according to Somali culture and Muslim religion it is a taboo for a woman to seek a political position. It sets a bad precedent.'*[142]

Sophia's eventual success lay in the fact that she was involved in running a branch of Womankind Kenya, which works closely with people at a grassroots level and which allowed her to become known and respected. Nevertheless, religious leaders in many northern areas of Kenya remain more influential than Members of Parliament, who come to rely on them to maintain support. This can give policies more of a conservative edge, particularly with regard to girls' education and FGM.[143] As Sophia Abdi Noor explains, the Qur'an continues to be interpreted to the detriment of women in northern Kenya:

> *'There is a Hadith of the Prophet that says a community led by a woman will be a bad omen … According to the Qur'an, a woman should not be a judge because her temperature and temperament changes prior to and during monthly periods; her judgment is unlikely to be fair. Second, a woman should not lead prayers in the mosque for the same reasons. This is why men pray five times and women are excused because of periods, pregnancy and childbirth.'*[144]

## Institutions

Customary domains of power within pastoralist societies have tended to formally segregate men and women. It seems that in the past there were often complementary institutions, but today only those belonging to men tend to survive.[145] In southern Ethiopia and northern Kenya the pan-Borana assembly, known as the *Gumii Gayyoo*, is held every eight years and is regarded as one of the most important events in the life of the community. NGOs and even the government itself use the assembly as an opportunity for advocacy among the Boran. However, women rarely attend or participate, except to testify about a specific event. Mumina Konso notes that:

> *'The first time a woman attended the meeting, she had no experience and was given only a few minutes to speak and then leave. All 150 men were facing the other way. "It is like talking to stones," she said.'*[146]

While most pastoralist women have informal authority over the actions and decisions of their husbands this does not amount to an institutionalized space for women. What a man says and does at an event such as the *Gumii Gayyoo* may well be influenced by his wife. But if women are unable to formally participate in public arenas within their own communities they are unlikely to participate in formal politics. Even among pastoralist associations that have been established through the intervention of NGOs, women continue to be largely absent, although even the inclusion and participation of a single woman can be seen as a notable success.[147] While governments have made provisions to include greater female and minority representation, there will be little change if this inequality is not addressed.

Of the four countries, Ethiopia has in principle gone further than any in recognizing its ethnic diversity and has gone so far as to offer self-determination to federated regional states. However, the Constitution does not stipulate a level of representation for women at any level of governance, and the level of regional autonomy remains severely curtailed under the authority of the federal government. It has also been suggested that a two-tier system of federalism has emerged, whereby the central highland states have gained greater political and economic development than the lowlands border regions of Afar, Benishangul-Gumuz, Gambella and Somali.[148] In practice, the ability of many of Ethiopia's pastoralist regions to govern themselves is minimal and pastoralist developments continue to be guided by a relatively centralized state.

Aneb Abdulkadir, from Ethiopia's Somali Region, explains the situation:

*'The local council is dominated by non-pastoralists and local people only have two or three councillors. The federal government still controls everything and political connections still interfere with autonomy. A decentralized system exists in Ethiopia but implementation is a problem. In village committees, 99.9 per cent are men. Only one or two women might be there. Yet it is the responsibility of the federal government to ensure women's participation.'* [149]

As has already been outlined, unlike the Ethiopian and Kenyan constitutions, which make no commitment to women's participation in the Parliament, the constitutions of both Tanzania and Uganda offer quotas and reservations that have increased women's participation. Winifred Masiko believes that the political and legal space that now exists allows women to compete. It is now up to women to decide to run.[150] The same sentiment is expressed in Kenya by Linah Jebii Kilimo:

*'Despite culture fighting the pastoralist woman, despite the lack of rights for women, there is still a space and it is that space that I tell women to exploit. Not as a feminist, saying that I want to do the work of a man; I just want to do the work that a man does the way a woman can. And that way I think I have been able to overcome.'* [151]

In Kenya, Tanzania and Uganda informal pastoral parliamentary groups have also been formed to spearhead pastoralist development, while in Ethiopia, a constitutionally mandated Pastoral Affairs Standing Committee was established in 2002 and provides oversight to a number of ministries. Prior to the disputed 2005 Ethiopian election, the Pastoral Affairs Standing Committee contained only male members. Today, there are three women, although appreciation of the issues facing pastoralist women appears to remain limited.[152]

In Kenya, the Pastoral Parliamentary Group was established as early as 1998 but it was not active until 2003. Women do not appear to be involved although lobbying by the group for affirmative action has been for both pastoralist and women's rights.[153] A group was formed in Uganda in 1999, but like the Kenyan group had to be relaunched in 2003, while the Tanzanian group was only formed in 2004.[154] Like all other political institutions, women are either absent or seem to have only limited involvement in the pastoral parliamentary groups and the Pastoral Affairs Standing Committee.

# What is being done?

Pastoralism in eastern Africa and the Horn has attracted a great deal of international attention over the last decade, though concern over pastoralist women has unfortunately lagged behind. The failure of policy-makers to recognize the roles and responsibilities of women has been blamed for the shortcomings of many livestock development projects.[155] Although governance has changed little since Markakis' observations in 2004, and there are still in general many policies aimed at sedentarization, there have been some recent alterations that could bring about a dramatic change in pastoralist development in the coming years. However, currently pastoralist rangelands are still often deemed more suitable for purposes other than pastoralism, which may ultimately force the abandonment of mobile livestock herding in some areas.

Opposing views are being heard from an increasingly vocal group of NGOs, which today includes a small number of organizations founded and led by pastoralist women themselves. These organizations are working to implement women's rights, strengthen livelihoods and to provide education and healthcare. In many instances, these efforts have included establishing women's groups and cooperatives, capacity-building, advocacy against FGM and promoting the role of pastoralist women as peacemakers. An increasingly supportive legislative environment is facilitating this work, although implementation remains woefully inadequate.

The priority is to continue advocating for the importance of pastoralism while building awareness of the challenges facing pastoralist women, in the hope of enabling these women to benefit fully from future development.

## Governance

The democratization process that has taken place throughout eastern Africa and the Horn has led to power being decentralized to federal or regional authorities and the recognition of greater diversity. This was evidenced most recently in Kenya when, on 30 April 2008, the Kenyan government launched the Ministry of Development of northern Kenya and Other Arid Lands. This was the first time that an entire government ministry had targeted pastoralist development in the region. The ministry now has a broad mandate to improve infrastructure, plan settlements, strengthen the livestock sector, manage natural resources, explore for minerals, establish tourism, and develop solar and wind power. Boaz Kaino, Member of Parliament for Marakwet West in northern Kenya, expresses his hopes:

> 'There is nothing to be proud about now, let us be frank, nothing has actually changed. But the government has started the Ministry of Northern Kenya and Other Arid Lands so if funding goes to that ministry and education is addressed, roads are addressed, and security is addressed then we can begin to see some light.' [156]

Granted a budget of 2.4 billion Kenyan Shillings, the new ministry is expected to focus on infrastructure development including roads, electricity and water supplies as well as abattoirs and tanneries, which it is hoped will stimulate the livestock economy.[157] However, pastoralist Members of Parliament had previously lobbied the government for 30 billion Kenyan Shillings as well as a commitment over the next ten years.[158] The three senior posts have been filled by men, while none of the prominent pastoralist women parliamentarians have been included.

These developments stand to build on the Kenyan government's Arid Lands Resource Management Project (ALARMP), which was initiated with funding from the World Bank. The project includes the construction of girls' dormitories and toilets in North Eastern Province in order to provide cleaner and safer learning environments. In addition, entrepreneurial training programmes for pastoralist women have also been initiated. Women are given key positions in committees and sub-committees at the community level and are furthermore encouraged to act as role models for female students.[159]

However, in many cases this process has gone even further and devolved authority over specific resources to customary institutions. In southern Ethiopia, the Borana Collaborative Forest Management Project was able to reinstate the community's customary authority over forest resources, which strengthened access rights and increased conservation. However, the project failed to assess the impact this would have on pastoralist women, who were only able to take up a limited number of positions at the lowest level of authority.[160] Conversely, in northern Kenya, famine relief provided to pastoralists in Turkana District tended to have a more positive effect on women, albeit one that was again unplanned:

*'Most of the men interviewed felt that "women" status in the family was uplifted as a result of the fact that they receive famine food relief. Many men interviewed however felt threatened by this because their role as providers was undervalued by the relief food controlled by women. This had brought conflict in some families.'* [161]

Although the impacts of these two interventions were quite different, in both cases greater recognition was needed that women's rights can be, and often are, curtailed just as quickly as new ones are beginning to be advocated for. Consequently, the customary institutions of women as well as those of men need to be identified. Although these may have been severely eroded, they nonetheless represent important avenues to overcoming marginalization and should be explored further before 'alternatives' are sought.

But despite these changes, government policy towards pastoralism has not altered significantly. Ethiopia, Kenya, Tanzania and Uganda all continue to implement large-scale rural transformation programmes. Tanzania's National Strategy for Growth and Poverty Reduction (2005–10) for instance, continues to treat pastoralists as of secondary importance and views their livelihoods as unsustainable. [162] Uganda's Plan for Modernization of Agriculture and Kenya's Vision 2030 also identify ways to exploit the resources held by pastoralists for the benefit of an export-orientated economy, while doing little to include them in the process. [163] In Ethiopia, a Livestock Development Master Plan is also being formulated. Michael Godwin Wantsusi of the Karamoja Agro-Pastoral Development Programme (KADP) shares the views of many:

*'Government programmes such as the Plan for Modernization of Agriculture are based on the notion of turning the lifestyle of agro-pastoralists into agriculturalists overnight. Such programmes fail to appreciate climatic, social and cultural realities on the ground that would provide a springboard for people-centred development and service delivery.'* [164]

Although it is arguable whether poverty or policy is the main force behind sedentarization, it continues to be encouraged by the state. [165] As evidenced earlier in this report, more sedentary lifestyles brought about by a shift to agro-pastoralism, land losses and environmental degradation have different impacts on men and women. As the Mkomazi case from Tanzania shows, this is not entirely negative as women can gain greater opportunities to be educated and to lead healthier lives. However, while sedentarization offers opportunities such as livelihood diversification and greater social freedoms, the reality is

that increased labour demands and impoverishment among pastoralists settled around urban centres has a largely negative impact on the lives of women. The situation in northern Kenya is indicative of the problem:

*'While settling in or near towns presents women with new opportunities, household poverty may prevent them from exploiting these opportunities or lead them to adopt environmentally unsustainable survival strategies that contribute to the localized degradation of the natural resource base.'* [166]

Sedentary pastoralist women have more difficulty accessing milk and milk products, as herds are increasingly being kept away at distant satellite camps. This severely limits redistribution between women in different households, compounding the poverty experienced by female headed households. In Tanzania, it is also suggested that as women have so little contact with the household's herds, their rights over animals given to them at marriage are entirely usurped by men who buy and sell without any regard for their wives' interests. [167]

## NGOs

The number of NGOs that address pastoralist development has increased dramatically in the last decade. A much smaller number have been established and run entirely by pastoralist women, and now provide crucial services to their own communities. These organizations are contributing to the debate on pastoralist development, which in the past tended to overlook the roles of women within the pastoralist economy. In many cases today, pastoralist women are being encouraged to diversify their incomes by forming savings and credit groups, and are being provided with access to educational opportunities and healthcare.

A common approach is that of the Karamoja Agro-Pastoral Development Programme (KADP) in Uganda. Established as an independent organization in 2003, KADP works in Moroto and Nakapiripirit districts of Karamoja Region. In addition to capacity-building, KADP has formed associations of community animal health workers (CAHW), women's goat groups, youth associations for young women and men, and councils of elders. Women have been empowered through these associations to exercise their rights over key household and community assets such as small livestock. As a result, women have begun to play more prominent roles in decision-making, as they have been encouraged to take up leadership roles in the new associations. [168]

In 1997 Maanda Ngoitika, a Maasai woman from Tanzania, began the Pastoral Women's Council (PWC) in order to mobilize Maasai women to claim their rights to land and education as well as increase participation in decision-making. Central to the work of PWC is education, which is provided both for women and children. The organization has also established a Women's Solidarity Boma, which provides a home and access to livestock for vulnerable women and their children. From these foundations, women are encouraged to assert their rights and voice them to government and NGOs. PWC also advocates against early marriage, a practice that the organization estimates causes three girls to abandon education every day.[169] Maanda Ngoitiko expresses the mission of PWC:

*'To start an organization like the Pastoral Women's Council needs long-term dedication, commitment and courage. We bring pastoralists together and give each other encouragement to break the cycle of silence and oppression.'*[170]

Similarly, in 1999 a group of four university-educated Pokot women in northern Kenya established Yang'at, which addresses issues affecting pastoralist girls. Targeting their efforts towards water, health and education, which were seen as key factors in determining the well-being of girls, Yang'at has today expanded and has reached 30,000 people with their interventions. Recently the group constructed six sub-surface dams in order to reduce the time taken to fetch water, which was achieved with community labour and resources. The time saved has allowed women and girls greater opportunities to attend school and to begin business ventures, for which Yang'at is also providing training.

In Ethiopia, the Afar Pastoral Development Association (APDA) has been providing social services since the mid-1990s in one of the most marginalized areas of the country. FGM is at the centre of all APDA's activities and is a practice that APDA believes can one day be eradicated. While federal laws that prohibit FGM remain unknown among the Afar, raising awareness about the complications of FGM with religious leaders has actually led to a dramatic change in some districts, as Valerie Browning of APDA explains:

*'The key to stopping FGM is to mobilize and give capacity to local Islamic leaders. The Qur'an says it should not be practised and when they understand that they are against their own religious teachings they stop. We then give FGM practitioners the opportunity to come in front of the Sheik and swear that they will give it up, which we have done for hundreds of women.'*[171]

APDA's approach highlights the need to include men in issues that affect only women. Although men do not per-

form FGM, they may sanction it through religion or through refusing to allow their sons to marry girls who have not been mutilated. In addition to these interventions, APDA also provides non-formal educational opportunities, with girls currently taking approximately 36 per cent of the class places. APDA's mission is to allow the Afar community to direct its own development, which will in turn empower women to become leaders.

While these are all important interventions, the general tendency to encourage group formation among pastoralists has not been as successful as its popularity would suggest. The economic benefits in particular are far from impressive.[172] Microfinance loans, savings and credit groups, and in particular legally recognized cooperatives, suffer multiple failures and there is a tendency to create dependency. Although there are different models of financial service associations being implemented among pastoralists Gufu Oba's observations are apt:

*'First, members divide interest earned from their loans as bonuses. Second, individuals are helped from group savings. Third, members of a group do not necessarily participate in each other's social security networks. Fourth, there is no evidence that groups encouraged women to advocate for their welfare any better than they did when they were using their indigenous social security networks. Fifth, such groups have poor leadership dynamics. Sixth, lack of political support undermines women's articulation on issues related to gender and decision-making processes.'*[173]

In addition, few pastoralist women's groups give FGM the same level of importance as many international NGOs and donors, choosing instead to focus on issues such as economic development. These groups have nonetheless succeeded on a number of occasions in empowering women socially, for instance through peace-building initiatives. Advocacy that stresses the links between FGM and the limitations placed on women's education and economic potential may help in this regard.

## Legislation

Laws have been enacted throughout eastern Africa and the Horn that are designed to protect and promote the rights of women as well as minorities. A number of international conventions and declarations have been signed by all four countries, including the Universal Declaration of Human Rights (1948), the International Convention on the Elimination of all Forms of Racial Discrimination (ICERD) (1969), the Convention on the Elimination of all Forms of Discrimination Against Women (CEDAW) (1979), the African Charter on

Human and Peoples' Rights (1981), the Convention on the Rights of the Child (1989), the African Charter on the Rights and Welfare of the Child (1990), the Beijing Platform for Action (1995) and the Protocol to the African Charter on Human and Peoples' Rights on the Rights of Women in Africa (2003).

In recent years, the introduction of national gender policies and legislative amendments which eliminate provisions that were discriminatory to women, have domesticated gender concerns. Ethiopia's National Policy on Women first came about in 1993, Kenya implemented its National Gender and Development Policy in 2000, Tanzania implemented its Women Development and Gender Policy in the same year and Uganda revised its Gender Policy in 2007.

Notable legal revisions include Ethiopia's Revised Family Code of 2000 that marked a significant step for women's rights in the country. It tightened legislation concerning consent in marriage and divorce rights, and criminalized FGM for the first time. Similarly, in Kenya, the Sexual Offences Bill came into force in 2006 and included 14 new offences ranging from gang rape to the deliberate transmission of HIV/AIDS. Gender equitable land legislation has also been introduced. The Ugandan Land Act (1998) for example nullifies any custom that prevents women from inheriting land and provides them with representation on all Land Committees and Tribunals. Furthermore, as has already been noted, Tanzania and Uganda both operate with reserved seats for women in the Parliament, and the ruling EPRDF party in Ethiopia has made a commitment to have a party quota of 30 per cent women.

While the existing legislation is not perfect, it does offer women far greater opportunities than ever before.[174] However, there is little to be gained from listing legislation that exists only on paper. It is widely documented that rural communities have not benefited from legal provisions and remain bound by customary practices. CEDAW country reports, for example, consistently question the inclusion of rural women throughout eastern Africa and the Horn, and they fail to mention pastoralists at all.[175] Governments now face the daunting challenge of implementing these provisions in provinces that are often remote and lack access to the media. This is further complicated due to the near constant securitization of many pastoralist regions because of conflict, which has served to undermine the rule of law in general.

As evidenced above, in Ethiopia's Afar Region laws prohibiting FGM are entirely unknown and prosecutions have never been sought. Change has come about because of raising awareness about the practice with religious leaders, which has led to the imprisonment of practitioners and fining the families of victims via *sharia* courts. These are only local initiatives and are unrelated to formal legislation. Although local initiatives are significant, implementation of formal legal provisions remains crucial, as Valerie Browning from APDA states:

*'There has to be a good family law, rights for women in marriage, rights in inheritance and so on. Then Afar women can come truly into their realm as leaders.'* [176]

Issues such as these are being addressed in Kenya through outreach work by KEWOPA that has allowed women parliamentarians to raise awareness about issues such as FGM to their constituents.[177] However, implementation remains extremely limited and few pastoralists can claim to know the rights afforded to them through national and international legislation. Women, in particular, have less access to the media or to policy-making. As a result they are less likely to participate fully in the opportunities being created by government and NGOs.

Specific practices that disproportionately affect the health and social status of women, such as FGM and early and forced marriages, need to be targeted. For interventions like these to be successful, they must include men, as they are often the ones who prescribe these procedures. This will also avoid a backlash against women suddenly seen to enforce rights with which men are unfamiliar. Increasing this awareness in pastoral areas where there is little access to social services or media is a significant challenge.

It must also be recognized that national legislation acts in tandem with religious and customary codes, which in pastoralist areas tend to have much greater authority. These continue to be discriminatory towards women, especially in terms of their marriage and inheritance rights. As a result, grassroots interventions that focus efforts on community leaders should begin any process of change. Outreach work carried out by pastoralist women parliamentarians and by NGOs working within the community are the best way to tackle these issues, rather than by top-down legislation that may have no effect on practices such as FGM on the ground.

# Conclusion

Pastoralism is not only a viable livelihood but also successfully conserves fragile natural resources and contributes significantly to national economies. However, with high population growth rates, reduction in livestock herds and restrictions on rangeland access all being exacerbated by climate change, those on the margins of the pastoralist economy are particularly vulnerable. More often than not these are women. Although women hold crucial roles in the pastoralist economy, they are also marginalized by institutions and policies both within their own communities and in wider governance. Pastoralism has a bright future in eastern Africa and the Horn, but only if the basis of women's marginalization is identified and addressed.

This report has highlighted some of the ways in which the marginalization of women and the marginalization of pastoralists intersect to leave pastoralist women extremely vulnerable. For example, public services such as education and healthcare have been shown to be chronically insufficient for pastoralists in general. However, women lag even further behind than men due to socio-cultural factors such as bridewealth and FGM. Pastoralist women also have extremely limited rights over resources despite legislation designed to offer them an equal footing.

In many instances the issues affecting pastoralist women are not being addressed at all while elsewhere interventions are not accorded the importance they deserve, thus they suffer from chronic under-funding and a lack of sustainability. The roles that pastoralists play in their wider national economies and societies in general, and the more specific responsibilities of pastoralist women, must be acknowledged. By doing so, livelihoods can be secured through appropriate developmental planning, which will allow fragile environmental resources to continue to be exploited in a sustainable manner.

Finally, we must conclude on a note of caution. Women from pastoralist societies are often portrayed as silent and subordinate individuals existing on the margins of an already marginal system. But they are far from helpless. As this report has tried to show, pastoralist women face multiple challenges in achieving their potential. However, some of them have been able to overcome these challenges and rise to prominent positions. Women such as Aneb Abdulkadir, Linah Jebii Kilimo, Maanda Ngoitika and many others embody that will and determination and are testimony to the potential of pastoralist women. Much remains to be done, but by providing access to the necessary skills, experiences and knowledge, pastoralist women can address the constraints on their participation themselves, and pastoralism can continue to thrive.

# Recommendations

## To the international community

- Treaty monitoring bodies, including ICERD and CEDAW, should highlight to states parties the marginalization experienced by pastoralist women and call for states parties to take action to fulfil their international legal obligations.
- Concerted pressure needs to be applied to governments in the region through the Human Rights Council to domesticate international treaties to which they are signatories. These already provide the broad framework through which women from minority groups can overcome marginalization, but suffer from a lack of political will and allocation of resources.

## To the governments of Ethiopia, Kenya, Tanzania and Uganda

- All international treaties must be fully implemented, in particular the Protocol to the African Charter on Human and Peoples' Rights on the Rights of Women in Africa.
- Electoral systems must be reviewed to ensure the fair representation of minority groups. Affirmative action measures should be explored in consultation with pastoralist communities and pastoralist women, and implemented to increase the number of pastoralist women.
- Health and educational services must be adapted to mobile households. Plans to do this must be drawn up in consultation with pastoralist communities and women, with adequate funding and clear deadlines.
- Universal primary education must be fully realized in pastoralist communities. Curricula that increase their skills and include subjects they value, such as veterinary skills, should be introduced
- Statistical data on pastoralists should be disaggregated between pastoralists and non-pastoralists, and between men and women. Pastoralist communities must also be included in any national census.

- The threat of HIV/AIDS to pastoralist communities and its impact on pastoralist women should be urgently assessed as a priority, and the determinants of transmission identified and addressed, as they have begun to be in other communities.
- Pastoralist communities should be valued as conservators of their environment. Policy-makers should embrace this international consensus and refocus efforts away from sedentarization.
- Policy-makers should refocus efforts currently concerned with sedentarization and work in closer collaboration with NGOs concerned with the future of pastoralism, in consultation with pastoralist women.
- Policies that revoke pastoralist rights to access and use natural resources without free, prior and informed consent and compensation should be abandoned.

## To NGOs and donor agencies

- Existing knowledge of pastoralist gender relations must be taken into account when developing pastoralist women's programmes.
- Statistical data on pastoralists should be disaggregated between pastoralists and non-pastoralists, and between men and women. This will highlight areas of acute marginalization and inherently strengthen the advocacy message.
- Negative attitudes towards girls' education must be advocated against and the value that an educated girl has needs to be exemplified.
- Parliamentary groups of both pastoralists and pastoralist women should be supported through experience-sharing, capacity-building and via financial assistance.
- Pastoralist women who become community leaders should be supported and promoted to help create positive role models within the community, educate wider society about pastoralism and help put pressure on governments.

# Notes

1  Markakis, J., *Pastoralism on the Margin*, London, MRG, 2004, pp. 7–10.
2  Hodgson, D.L., 'Gender, culture and the myth of the patriarchal pastoralist', in D.L. Hodgson (ed.), *Rethinking Pastoralism in Africa: Gender, Culture and the Myth of the Patriarchal Pastoralist*, Oxford, James Currey, 2000.
3  Morton, J., Livingstone, J.K. and Mussa, M., *Legislators and Livestock: Pastoralist Parliamentary Groups in Ethiopia, Kenya and Uganda*, Gatekeeper Series 131, London, International Institute for Environment and Development, 2007, pp. 13–14.
4  Markakis, *op. cit.*, pp. 11–13.
5  Hodgson, *op. cit.*, pp. 1–2.
6  *Ibid.*, pp. 17–18.
7  Interviews by Andrew Ridgewell with Hon. Linah Jebii Kilimo, Chair of the Kenya Women Parliamentary Association (KEWOPA), Kenya, 13 June 2008, and Hon. Anchinalu Yigzaw, Chair of the Women's Affairs Standing Committee, Ethiopia, 2 July 2008.
8  See, for example, the collection contained in Kipuri, N., *Oral Literature of the Maasai*, Nairobi, Heinemann, 1983.
9  Interview by Naomi Kipuri with Clementina Meteyian, Tanzania, 21 July 2007.
10  Elmi, A.H., Ibrahim, D. and Jenner, J., 'Women's roles in peacemaking in Somali society', in D.L. Hodgson (ed.), *Rethinking Pastoralism in Africa: Gender, Culture and the Myth of the Patriarchal Pastoralist*, Oxford, James Currey, 2000, p. 124.
11  Kipuri, N., 'Maasai women in transition: class and gender in the transformation of a pastoral society', unpublished PhD thesis, Temple University, Philadelphia, PA, 1989, p. 179.
12  One of the few pieces of research to deal with alcohol production and consumption among pastoralists can be found in Holtzman, J., 'The food of elders, the "ration" of women: brewing, gender, and domestic processes among the Samburu of northern Kenya', *American Anthropologist*, vol. 103, no. 4, 2001.
13  The leaves of the *Catha Edulis* tree contain cathine and cathonine that act as a mild stimulant to the user. They also represent a major export, although a growing number of countries in the West have moved to ban their use.
14  Devereux, S., *Vulnerable Livelihoods in Somali Region, Ethiopia*, Brighton, Institute of Development Studies, 2006, pp. 123–4.
15  Interview by Naomi Kipuri with Denebo Dekeba, Gudina Tumsa Foundation, Ethiopia, 15 August 2007.
16  Interview by Naomi Kipuri with Bono Belante, Ethiopia, 20 August 2007.
17  Markakis, *op. cit.*, p. 12.
18  Coast, E., 'Maasai marriage: a comparative study of Kenya and Tanzania', *Journal of Comparative Family Studies*, vol. 37, no. 3, 2006, p. 402.
19  Mburu, N., 'The proliferation of guns and rustling in Karamoja and Turkana Districts: the case for appropriate disarmament strategies', *Peace, Conflict and Development*, vol. 2, no. 1, 2002, p. 10.
20  Interview by Naomi Kipuri with Juliana Auma, Uganda, 25 July 2007.
21  Interview by Naomi Kipuri with Oscar Okech, African Leadership Institute, Uganda, 24 July 2007.
22  Interview by Naomi Kipuri with Hon. Aneb Abdulkadir, Ethiopia, 15 August 2007.
23  See Moore, T. and Mohammed, A., 'Gender-based violence in Afar', unpublished report for SOS Sahel Ethiopia's Gender and Pastoralism Research Project.
24  Interview by Naomi Kipuri with Honey Hassan, Ethopia, 17 August 2007.
25  Stites, E., Akabwai, D., Mazurana, D. and Ateyo, P., *Angering Akujü: Survival and Suffering in Karamoja, A Report on Livelihoods and Human Security in the Karamoja Region of Uganda*, Medford, MA, Feinstein International Center, Tufts University, 2007, p. 53.
26  Moore and Mohammed, *op. cit.*
27  Wawire, V.K., *Gender and the Social and Economic Impacts of Drought on the Residents of Turkana District in Northern Kenya*, Addis Ababa, Organization for Social Science Research in Eastern and Southern Africa (OSSREA), 2003, p. 22.
28  Interview with Juliana Auma, *op. cit.*
29  Lydall, J., 'The power of women in an ostensibly male-dominated agro-pastoral society', in T. Widlok and Gossa Tadesse (eds), *Property and Equality, vol. 2: Encapsulation, Commercialization, Discrimination*, Oxford, Berghahn, 2005, pp. 154–72.
30  Moore and Mohammed, *op. cit.*
31  Interview by Naomi Kipuri with Hon. Sophia Abdi Noor, Kenya, 6 July 2007.
32  Spencer, P., *The Maasai of Matapato: A Study of Rituals and Rebellion*, Bloomington, Indiana University Press, 1988, p. 205.
33  See Kuwee Kumsa, 'The Siiqqee institution of Oromo women', *Journal of Oromo Studies*, vol. 4, no. 1/2, 1997.
34  Watson, E., 'Inter-institutional alliances and conflicts in natural resource management: preliminary research findings from Borana, Oromia Region, Ethiopia', Working Paper 4, Brighton, Marena Research Project, 2000, p. 14.
35  Holtzman, J., 'Politics and gastropolitics: gender and the power of food in two African pastoralist societies', *Journal of the Royal Anthropological Institute*, vol. 8, no. 2, 2002, pp. 269–71.
36  Sagawa, T., 'Wives' domestic and political activities at home: the space of coffee drinking among the Daasanetch of Southwestern Ethiopia', *African Study Monographs*, vol. 27, no. 2, 2006, p. 72.
37  Devereux, *op. cit.*, p. 155.
38  Leggett, I., 'Learning to improve education policy for pastoralists in Kenya', in S. Aikman and E. Unterhalter (eds), *Beyond Access: Transforming Policy and Practice for Gender Equality in Education*, Oxford, Oxfam, 2005, p. 131.
39  Stites *et al.*, *op. cit.*, p. 14, citing World Food Program, *Emergency Food Security Assessment, Karamoja Region, Kampala* (July 2007).
40  Kimesera, N. and Hodgson, D.L., 'In the shadow of the MDGs: pastoralist women and children in Tanzania', *Indigenous Affairs*, no. 1, 2006, p. 33.
41  Carr-Hill, R., Eshete, A., Sedel, C. and de Souza, A., *The Education of Nomadic Peoples in East Africa: Djibouti, Eritrea, Ethiopia, Kenya, Tanzania and Uganda*, Paris, UNESCO, 2005, pp. 69–70; Leggett, *op. cit.*, p. 129.
42  Nyamongo, I.K., 'Factors influencing education and age at first marriage in an arid region: the case of the Borana of Marsabit District, Kenya', *African Study Monographs*, vol. 21, no. 2, 2000, p. 62.
43  Interview with Linah Jebii Kilimo, *op. cit.*

44  Leggett, *op. cit.*, pp. 136–7.
45  Interview by Andrew Ridgewell with Michael Godwin Wantsusi, Karamoja Agro-Pastoral Development Programme (KADP), Uganda, 4 July 2008.
46  'Why the classroom still eludes Karimojong girls', *New Vision* (Kampala), 10 September 2006.
47  *Ibid.*
48  Morton *et al.*, *op. cit.*, p. 12.
49  Interview by Naomi Kipuri with Margaret Aleper Achila, Women's Representative for Kotido District, Ethiopia, 17 August 2007.
50  Devereux, *op. cit.*, pp. 120–3.
51  Stites *et al.*, *op. cit.*, p. 14, citing Walker (2002)
52  Coast, E., 'Maasai demography', unpublished PhD thesis, University of London, 2000, pp. 99–109.
53  Mace, R. and Sear, R., 'Maternal mortality in a Kenyan pastoralist population', *International Journal of Gynecology and Obstetrics*, vol. 54, no. 2, 1996, p. 140.
54  Stites *et al.*, *op. cit.*, p. 14, citing United Nations (2007).
55  Coast, 'Maasai demography', *op. cit.*, p. 14.
56  Mason, C., 'Camps, cholera and cattle raids', *Canadian Medical Association Journal*, vol. 178, no. 2, 2008, pp. 133–5.
57  Morton, J., 'Conceptualising the links between HIV/AIDS and pastoralist livelihoods', *European Journal of Development Research*, vol. 18, no. 2, 2006, p. 242.
58  *Ibid.*, p. 248.
59  Lydall, J., 'The threat of the HIV/AIDS epidemic in South Omo Zone, southern Ethiopia', *Northeast African Studies*, vol. 7, no. 1, 2000, p. 46.
60  Coast, E., 'Wasting semen: context and condom use among the Maasai', *Cultural, Health and Sexuality*, vol. 9, no. 4, 2007, p. 395.
61  Morton, *op. cit.*, p. 244.
62  Coast, 'Maasai demography', *op. cit.*, p. 395; Talle, A., '"Serious games": licences and prohibitions in Maasai sexual life', *Africa*, vol. 77, no. 3, 2007, p. 362.
63  Talle, *op. cit.*, pp. 358–60.
64  Lydall, 'The threat of the HIV/AIDS epidemic …', *op. cit.*, p. 44.
65  Talle, A., 'Pastoralists at the border: Maasai poverty and the development discourse in Tanzania', in D. Anderson and V. Broch-Due (eds), *The Poor Are Not Us: Poverty and Pastoralism in Eastern Africa*, Oxford, James Currey, 1999, pp. 120–1; Brockington, D., 'Women's income and the livelihood strategies of dispossessed pastoralists near the Mkomazi Game Reserve, Tanzania', *Human Ecology*, vol. 29, no. 3, 2001, p. 329; Devereux, *op. cit.*, p. 57; Mkutu, K.A., 'Uganda: pastoral conflict and gender relations', *Review of African Political Economy*, vol. 35, no. 2, 2008, p. 248.
66  Lydall, 'The threat of the HIV/AIDS epidemic …', *op. cit.*, p. 46; Middleton, J., 'Aspects of tourism in Kenya', *Anthropology Southern Africa*, vol. 27, no. 3/4, 2004, p. 71.
67  Coast, E., 'Local understandings of, and responses to, HIV: rural–urban migrants in Tanzania', *Social Science & Medicine*, vol. 63, no. 4, 2006, pp. 1000–10.
68  Brewer, D.D., Potterat, J.J., Roberts, J.M. Jr and Brody, S., 'Male and female circumcision associated with prevalent HIV infection in virgins and adolescents in Kenya, Lesotho, and Tanzania', *Annals of Epidemiology*, vol. 17, no. 3, 2007, pp. 217–26.
69  Interview with Linah Jebii Kilimo, *op. cit.*
70  Interview by Naomi Kipuri with Everlyn Chemtai, Uganda, 26 July 2007.
71  'Sabiny now circumcise married women', *New Vision* (Kampala), 9 December 2003.
72  Interview by Naomi Kipuri with Peris Tobiko, Kenya, 6 July 2007.
73  Interview with Sophia Abdi Noor, *op. cit.*
74  Interview with Linah Jebii Kilimo, *op. cit.*
75  Interview by Andrew Ridgewell with Hon. Winifred Masiko, Chair of the Uganda Women Parliamentary Association (UWOPA), Uganda, 10 July 2008.
76  Hodgson, *op. cit.*, p. 11.
77  Lydall, 'The power of women …', *op. cit.*, p. 171.
78  Interview by Naomi Kipuri with two Hamar women in Jinka, Ethiopia, 19 August 2007.
79  Interview by Naomi Kipuri with Paulina Tipap, Addis Ababa, 18 August 2007.
80  Hodgson, *op. cit.*, p. 10.
81  Markakis, *op. cit.*, p. 12.
82  Doss, C. and McPeak, J., 'Are household production decisions cooperative? Evidence on pastoral migration and milk sales from northern Kenya', *Yale University Economic Growth Center Discussion Paper 906*, New Haven, CT, Yale University, 2005, p. 3.
83  Kipuri, 'Maasai women in transition …', *op. cit.*, p. 179.
84  Birch, I. and Shuria, H.A.O., 'Taking charge of the future: pastoral institution building in northern Kenya', Drylands Issue Paper 114, London, International Institute for Environment and Development, 2002, p. 16; Osterloh, S., 'Rectifying distributionally regressive microfinance systems in northern Kenya', *Global Livestock CRSP Research Brief* 04-10-PARIMA, 2004, pp. 2–3.
85  The framework for establishing a total economic valuation of pastoralism is outlined in Hesse, C. and MacGregor, J., 'Pastoralism: drylands' invisible asset? Developing a framework for assessing the value of pastoralism in East Africa', Drylands Issue Paper 142, London, International Institute for Environment and Development, 2006.
86  See the discussions contained in Hatfield, R. and Davies, J., *Global Review of the Economics of Pastoralism*, Nairobi, International Union for Conservation and Nature, 2006.
87  Watson, *op. cit.*, p. 14.
88  Markakis, *op. cit.*, p. 21.
89  Interview by Naomi Kipuri with James Getaru, Tanzania, 19 July 2007.
90  Interview with Denebo Dekeba, *op. cit.*
91  'Basongora evicted from National Park', *New Vision* (Kampala), 23 September 2007.
92  'Basongora have always been a persecuted tribe', *New Vision* (Kampala), 9 July 2007.
93  'Ethio-Korean farm privatised, sweet 16', *Addis Fortune* (Addis Ababa), 15 April 2007; 'Italian firm begins development of palm oil investment', *Addis Fortune* (Addis Ababa), 17 June 2007.
94  'Wildlife and livelihoods at risk in Kenyan wetlands biofuel project', *The Guardian* (London), 24 June 2008.
95  Lesorogol, C.K., 'Transforming institutions among pastoralists: inequality and land privatization', *American Anthropologist*, vol. 105, no. 3, 2003, p. 535.
96  Brockington, *op. cit.*, p. 332.
97  See Smith, K., 'Sedentarization and market integration: new opportunities for Rendille and Ariaal women of northern Kenya', *Human Organization*, vol. 57, no. 4, 1998.
98  Interviews by Naomi Kipuri with Rebecca Lolosooli, a Samburu woman from Kenya, and Eunice Marima, a Maasai woman from Kenya, Ethiopia, 18 August 2007.
99  Aboud, A.A., Kisoyan, P.K. and Layne Coppock, D., 'Agro-pastoralists' wrath for the prosopis tree: the case of the Il Chamus of Baringo District, Kenya', *Global Livestock CRSP Research Brief* 05-02-PARIMA, 2005, p. 2.
100  Personal observations by Naomi Kipuri and discussions with the Community Research and Development Services, Tanzania, 16 July 2007.
101  Melesse Getu, 'Local versus outsider forms of natural resources use and management: the Tsamako experience of southwest Ethiopia', in K. Fukai, E. Kurimoto and M. Shigeta (eds) *Ethiopia in Broader Perspective*, vol. 2, Kyoto, Shokado, 1997, p. 761.

102 United Nations Convention to Combat Desertification (UNCCD) *Women Pastoralists: Preserving Traditional Knowledge, Facing Modern Challenges*, Bonn, Secretariat of UNCCD and the International Fund for Agricultural Development, 2007, p. 14.

103 Mulugeta Lemenih, Tarkegn Abebe and Olsson, M., 'Gum and resin resources from some Acacia, Boswellia and Commiphora species and their economic contributions in Liban, south-east Ethiopia', *Journal of Arid Environments*, no. 55, 2003, p. 475; Egadu, S.P., Mucunguzi, P. and Obua, J., 'Uses of tree species producing gum arabic in Karamoja, Uganda', *African Journal of Ecology*, vol. 45, supplement 1, 2007, pp. 19–20.

104 UNCCD, *op. cit.*, pp. 26–7.

105 Mwangi, M., 'Gender and drought hazards in the rangelands of the Great Horn of Africa: is gender equity the only solution?', *Women and Environments* spring/summer 2007, p. 22.

106 Wawire, *op. cit.*, p. 13.

107 Mwangi, *op. cit.*, p. 23.

108 Oba, G., 'The importance of pastoralists' indigenous coping strategies for planning drought management in the arid zone of Kenya', *Nomadic Peoples*, vol. 5, no. 1, 2001, p. 101.

109 Yohannes Gebre Michael, Kassaye Hadgu and Zerihun Ambaye, *Addressing Pastoralist Conflict in Ethiopia: The Case of the Kuraz and Hamer Sub-Districts of South Omo Zone*, Nairobi, Africa Peace Forum, 2005, p. 25; Mkutu, *op. cit.*, p. 242.

110 Watson, C., *Pastoral Women as Peacemakers*, Nairobi, Community Based Animal Health and Participatory Epidemiology Unit of the African Union/Interafrican Bureau for Animal Resources, 2003, p. 11.

111 Stites *et al.*, *op. cit.*, p. 59.

112 Interview with Denebo Dekeba, *op. cit.*

113 Watson, *op. cit.*, p. 15.

114 Interview by Andrew Ridgewell with Hon. Boaz K. Kaino, Kenya, 12 June 2008 and Oscar Oketch, *op. cit.*

115 Mkutu, *op. cit.*, p. 246.

116 Interview with Oscar Oketch, *op. cit.*

117 See Elmi, Ibrahim and Jenner, *op. cit.*

118 Nation, F., 'Wajir peace initiative – Kenya: back to the future dialogue and communication', *Conflict Prevention Newsletter*, vol. 2, no. 1, 1999, pp. 4–5.

119 Interview by Naomi Kipuri with Allyce Kureyia, Tanzania, 19 July 2007.

120 Data from the Inter-Parliamentary Union, as of 30 April 2008, URL (retrieved October 2008): http://www.ipu.org/wmn-e/classif.htm

121 'Parliament failed major affirmative action test', *East African Standard* (Nairobi), 22 August 2007.

122 'Women MPs miss out on key teams', *The Nation* (Nairobi), 1 May 2008.

123 Interviews by Andrew Ridgewell with Winifred Maskio and Michael Godwin Wantsusi, *op. cit.* Florence Adong Omwony won the by-election for Ladwor County, now called Thur, in January 2008 following the death of the incumbent, her husband, Omwony Ojwok.

124 Interview with Winifred Masiko, *op. cit.*

125 The current Women's Representatives for Karamoja's five districts are: Janet Grace Akech Okori-Moe (Abim); Christine Tubbo Nakwang (Kaabong); Margaret Alepar Achila (Kotido); Stella Namoe (Moroto); and Rose Iriama (Nakapiripirit).

126 'Minority tribes want MPs', *New Vision* (Kampala), 10 June 2008.

127 Interview with Winifred Masiko, *op. cit*; Goetz, A.M., 'No shortcuts to power: constraints on women's political effectiveness in Uganda', *Journal of Modern African Studies*, vol. 40, no. 4, 2002, pp. 557–9.

128 Morna, C.L., 'Beyond numbers – quotas in practice', paper presented at the conference 'The Implementation of Quotas: African Experiences', Pretoria, 11–12 November 2003, p. 7.

129 'A break with tradition sees Mogotio get woman MP', *The Nation* (Nairobi), 6 January 2008.

130 'Parties reach out to "marginalised" areas as they nominate their MPs', *The Nation* (Nairobi), 22 March 2008.

131 Devereux, *op. cit.*, p. 119.

132 Interview by Naomi Kipuri with Maria Endagaw, Tanzania, 19 July 2007.

133 Interview by Naomi Kipuri with Mumina Konso, Ethiopia, 2 August 2007.

134 Interview with Linah Jebii Kilimo, *op. cit.*

135 Interviews with Linah Jebii Kilimo and Winifred Masiko, *op. cit.*

136 Interview by Naomi Kipuri with Tiyah Galgalo, Kenya, 6 July 2007.

137 Interview by Naomi Kipuri with the Member of Parliament for Kajiado Central, Kenya, July 2007.

138 Interview with Winifred Masiko, *op. cit.*

139 *Ibid.*

140 Interview by Naomi Kipuri with Ndinini Kimesera Sikar, Tanzania, 9 August 2007.

141 Interview by Naomi Kipuri with Eunice Marima, Kenya, 17 August 2007.

142 Interview with Sophia Abdi Noor, *op. cit.*

143 Livingstone, J., 'A comparative study of pastoralist parliamentary groups: Kenya case study', unpublished report prepared for the NRI/PENHA Research Project on Pastoralist Parliamentary Groups, 2005, p. 32.

144 Interview with Sophia Abdi Noor, *op. cit.*

145 Stites *et al.*, *op. cit.*, p. 16; Kuwee Kumsa, *op. cit.*, p. 115.

146 Interview with Mumina Konso, *op. cit.*

147 Birch and Shuria, *op. cit.*, p. 16.

148 Young, J., 'Along Ethiopia's western frontier: Gambella and Benishangul in transition', *Journal of Modern African Studies*, vol. 37, no. 2, 1999, p. 344.

149 Interview with Aneb Abdulkadir, *op. cit.*

150 Interview with Winifred Masiko, *op. cit.*

151 Interview with Linah Jebii Kilimo, *op. cit.*

152 Interview by Andrew Ridgewell with Hon. Awoke Aike, Chair of the Pastoral Affairs Standing Committee, 20 June 2008.

153 Livingstone, *op. cit.*, p. 45.

154 Morton *et al.*, *op. cit.*, pp. 8–9.

155 Hodgson, *op. cit.*, p. 10.

156 Interview with Boaz K. Kaino, *op. cit.*

157 'Northern Kenya wins sh2bn budget support', *Business Daily* (Nairobi), 16 June 2008.

158 'Northern Region ministry needs sh30bn, say MPs', *East African Standard* (Nairobi), 1 May 2008.

159 Arid Lands Resource Management Project Phase 2, Progress Report for the Period 2003–2006, Nairobi, Government of Kenya, Department of Special Programmes, 2006, p. 48.

160 Getachew Mamo, '"Community" forest management in Borana?', in A. Ridgewell, Getachew Mamo and F. Flintan (eds), *Gender and Pastoralism, vol. 1: Rangeland and Resource Management in Ethiopia*, Addis Ababa, SOS Sahel Ethiopia, 2007, pp. 28–9.

161 Wawire, *op. cit.*, p. 14.

162 Kipuri, N. and Sørensen, C., *Poverty, Pastoralism and Policy in Ngorongoro: Lessons Learned from the Ereto 1 Ngorongoro Pastoralist Project with Implications for Pastoral Development and the Policy Debate*, London, International Institute for Environment and Development, 2008, p. 4.

163 Odhiambo, M.O., 'Is education a licence to exploit the people?', *Haramata*, vol. 53, 2008, p. 12.

164 Interview with Michael Godwin Wantsusi, *op. cit.*.

165 Markakis, *op. cit.*, p. 13.

166 Nduma, I., Kristjanson, P. and McPeak, J., 'Diversity in income-generating activities for sedentarized pastoral women in northern Kenya', *Human Organization*, vol. 60, no. 4, 2001, p. 319.

167 Mung'ong'o, C.G., 'Social transformation and political empowerment in the age of globalization: looking beyond women's empowerment in Tanzania', *Nordic Journal of African Studies*, vol. 12, no. 2, 2003, pp. 126–7.

168 Interview with Michael Godwin Wantsusi, *op. cit.*

169 'In Tanzania, a Maasai girl escapes to education', *Reuters* (Arusha), 29 January 2008.

170 Interview by Andrew Ridgewell with Maanda Ngoitiko, Pastoral Women's Council (PWC), Tanzania, 30 June 2008.

171 Interview by Andrew Ridgewell with Valerie Browning, Afar Pastoral Development Association (APDA), Ethiopia, 26 June 2008.

172 Osterloh, *op. cit.*, pp. 2–3.

173 Oba, *op. cit.*, p. 105.

174 Interviews with Winifred Masiko, Linah Jebii Kilimo and Anchinalu Yigzaw, *op. cit.*

175 'Initial, Second and Third Period Reports of States Parties, Ethiopia', p. 21; 'Third and Fourth Periodic Reports of State Parties, Kenya', p. 35; 'Combined Fourth, Fifth and Six Periodic Reports of States Parties, Tanzania', pp. 20–21; 'Third Periodic Reports of States Parties' Uganda', pp. 56–9.

176 Interview with Valerie Browning, *op. cit.*

177 Interview with Linah Jebii Kilimo, *op. cit.*

# Bibliography

Surnames are not used in Ethiopia and an individual's personal name is followed by that of his or her father (and more recently grandfather). Thus Ethiopian authors are not referenced using standard formats but rather under their given names.

Aboud, A.A., Kisoyan, P.K. and Coppock, D.L., 'Agro-pastoralists' wrath for the prosopis tree: the case of the Il Chamus of Baringo District, Kenya', *Global Livestock CRSP Research Brief* 05-02-PARIMA, 2005.

Birch, I. and Shuria, H.A.O., 'Taking charge of the future: pastoral institution building in northern Kenya', Drylands Issue Paper 114, London, International Institute for Environment and Development, 2002.

Brewer, D.D., Potterat, J.J., Roberts, Jr, J.M. and Brody, S., 'Male and female circumcision associated with prevalent HIV infection in virgins and adolescents in Kenya, Lesotho, and Tanzania', *Annals of Epidemiology*, vol. 17, no. 3, 2007, pp. 217–26.

Brockington, D., 'Women's income and the livelihood strategies of dispossessed pastoralists near the Mkomazi Game Reserve, Tanzania', *Human Ecology*, vol. 29, no. 3, 2001, pp. 307–38.

Carr-Hill, R., Eshete, A., Sedel, C. and de Souza, A., *The Education of Nomadic Peoples in East Africa: Djibouti, Eritrea, Ethiopia, Kenya, Tanzania and Uganda*, Synthesis Report, Paris, UNESCO, 2005.

Coast, E., 'Maasai demography', unpublished PhD Thesis, University of London, 2000.

Coast, E., 'Local understandings of, and responses to, HIV: rural–urban migrants in Tanzania', *Social Science & Medicine*, vol. 63, no. 4, 2006, pp. 1000–10.

Coast, E., 'Maasai marriage: a comparative study of Kenya and Tanzania', *Journal of Comparative Family Studies*, vol. 37, no. 3, 2006, pp. 399–419.

Coast, E., 'Wasting semen: context and condom use among the Maasai', *Cultural, Health and Sexuality*, vol. 9, no. 4, 2007, pp. 387–401.

Devereux, S., *Vulnerable Livelihoods in Somali Region, Ethiopia*, Brighton, Institute of Development Studies, 2006.

Doss, C.R. and McPeak, J.G., 'Are household production decisions cooperative? Evidence on pastoral migration and milk sales from northern Kenya', *Yale University Economic Growth Center Discussion Paper 906*, New Haven, CT, Yale University, 2005.

Egadu, S.P., Mucunguzi, P. and Obua, J., 'Uses of tree species producing gum arabic in Karamoja, Uganda', *African Journal of Ecology*, vol. 45, supplement 1, 2007, pp. 17–21.

Elmi, A.H., Ibrahim D. and Jenner, J., 'Women's roles in peacemaking in Somali society', in D. Hodgson (ed.), *Rethinking Pastoralism in Africa: Gender, Culture and the Myth of the Patriarchal Pastoralist*, Oxford, James Currey, 2000, pp. 121–41.

Getachew Mamo, '"Community" forest management in Borana?', in A. Ridgewell, Getachew Mamo and F. Flintan (eds), *Gender and Pastoralism, vol. 1: Rangeland and Resource Management in Ethiopia*, Addis Ababa, SOS Sahel Ethiopia, 2007, pp. 15–32.

Goetz, A.M., 'No shortcuts to power: constraints on women's political effectiveness in Uganda', *Journal of Modern African Studies*, vol. 40, no. 4, 2002, pp. 549–75.

Hatfield, R. and Davies, J., *Global Review of the Economics of Pastoralism*, Nairobi, International Union for Conservation and Nature, 2006.

Hesse, C. and MacGregor, J., 'Pastoralism: drylands' invisible asset? Developing a framework for assessing the value of pastoralism in East Africa', Drylands Issue Paper 142, London, International Institute for Environment and Development, 2006.

Hodgson, D.L., 'Gender, culture and the myth of the patriarchal pastoralist', in D. Hodgson (ed.), *Rethinking Pastoralism in Africa: Gender, Culture and the Myth of the Patriarchal Pastoralist*, Oxford, James Currey, 2000a, pp. 1–28.

Holtzman, J., 'The food of elders, the "ration" of women: brewing, gender, and domestic processes among the Samburu of northern Kenya', *American Anthropologist*, vol. 103, no. 4, 2001, pp. 1041–58.

Holtzman, J., 'Politics and gastropolitics: gender and the power of food in two African pastoralist societies', *Journal of the Royal Anthropological Institute*, vol. 8, no. 2, 2002, pp. 259–78.

Kipuri, N., *Oral Literature of the Maasai*, Nairobi, Heinemann, 1983.

Kipuri, N., 'Maasai women in transition: class and gender in the transformation of a pastoral society', unpublished PhD thesis, Temple University, Philadelphia, PA, 1989.

Kipuri, N. and Sørensen, C., *Poverty, Pastoralism and Policy in Ngorongoro: Lessons Learned from the Ereto 1 Ngorongoro Pastoralist Project with Implications for Pastoral Development and the Policy Debate*, London, International Institute for Environment and Development, 2008.

Kuwee Kumsa, 'The siiqqee institution of Oromo women', *Journal of Oromo Studies*, vol. 4, no. 1/2, 1997, pp. 115–52.

Leggett, I., 'Learning to improve education policy for pastoralists in Kenya', in S. Aikman and E. Unterhalter (eds), *Beyond Access: Transforming Policy and Practice for Gender Equality in Education*, Oxford, Oxfam, 2005, pp. 128–48.

Lesorogol, C.K., 'Transforming institutions among pastoralists: inequality and land privatization', *American Anthropologist*, vol. 105, no. 3, 2003, pp. 531–41.

Livingstone, J., 'A comparative study of pastoralist parliamentary groups: Kenya case study', unpublished report prepared for the NRI/PENHA Research Project on Pastoralist Parliamentary Groups, 2005.

Lowe Morna, C., 'Beyond numbers – quotas in practice', paper presented at the conference 'The Implementation of Quotas: African Experiences', Pretoria, 11–12 November 2003.

Lydall, J., 'The threat of the HIV/AIDS epidemic in South Omo Zone, southern Ethiopia', *Northeast African Studies*, vol. 7, no. 1, 2000, pp. 41–62.

Lydall, J., 'The power of women in an ostensibly male-dominated agro-pastoral society', in T. Widlok and W. Gossa Tadesse (eds), *Property and Equality, vol. 2: Encapsulation, Commercialization, Discrimination*, Oxford, Berghahn, 2005, pp. 152–72.

Mace, R. and Sear, R., 'Maternal mortality in a Kenyan pastoralist population', *International Journal of Gynecology and Obstetrics*, vol. 54, no. 2, 1996, pp. 137–41.

Markakis, J., *Pastoralism on the Margin*, London, MRG, 2004.

Mason, C., 'Camps, cholera and cattle raids', *Canadian Medical Association Journal*, vol. 178, no. 2, 2008, pp. 133–5.

Mburu, N., 'The proliferation of guns and rustling in Karamoja and Turkana Districts: the case for appropriate disarmament strategies', *Peace, Conflict and Development*, vol. 2, no. 1, 2002.

Melesse Getu, 'Local versus outsider forms of natural resource management: the Tsamako experience in southwest Ethiopia', in K. Fukai, E. Kurimoto and M. Shigeta (eds), *Ethiopia in Broader Perspective*, vol. 2, Kyoto, Shokado, 1997, pp. 748–68.

Middleton, J., 'Aspects of tourism in Kenya', *Anthropology Southern Africa*, vol. 27, no. 3/4, 2004, pp. 65–74.

Mkutu, K.A., 'Uganda: pastoral conflict and gender relations', *Review of African Political Economy*, vol. 35, no. 2, 2008, pp. 237–54.

Morton, J., 'Conceptualising the links between HIV/AIDS and pastoralist livelihoods', *European Journal of Development Research*, vol. 18, no. 2, 2006, pp. 235–54.

Morton, J., Livingstone, J.K. and Mussa, M., *Legislators and Livestock: Pastoralist Parliamentary Groups in Ethiopia, Kenya and Uganda*, Gatekeeper Series 131, London, International Institute of Environment and Development, 2007.

Mulugeta Lemenih, Tarakegn Abebe and Olsson, M., 'Gum and resin resources from some Acacia, Boswellia and Commiphora species and their economic contributions in Liban, south-east Ethiopia', *Journal of Arid Environments*, vol. 55, 2003, pp. 465–82.

Mung'ong'o, C.G., 'Social transformation and political empowerment in the age of globalization: looking beyond women's empowerment in Tanzania', *Nordic Journal of African Studies*, vol. 12, no. 2, 2003, pp. 119–33.

Mwangi, M., 'Gender and drought hazards in the rangelands of the Great Horn of Africa: is gender equity the only solution?', *Women and Environments*, spring/summer, 2007, pp. 21–24.

Nation, F., 'Wajir peace initiative – Kenya: back to the future dialogue and communication', *Conflict Prevention Newsletter*, vol. 2, no. 1, 1999, pp. 4–5.

Nduma, I., Kristjanson, P. and McPeak, J., 'Diversity in income-generating activities for sedentarized pastoral women in northern Kenya', *Human Organization*, vol. 60, no. 4, 2001, pp. 319–25.

Nyamongo, I.K., 'Factors influencing education and age at first marriage in an arid region: the case of the Borana of Marsabit District, Kenya', *African Study Monographs*, vol. 21, no. 2, 2000, pp. 55–65.

Oba, G., 'The importance of pastoralists' indigenous coping strategies for planning drought management in the arid zone of Kenya', *Nomadic Peoples*, vol. 5, no. 1, 2001, pp. 89–119.

Ochieng Odhiambo, M., 'Is education a license to exploit the people?', *Haramata*, vol. 53, 2008, pp. 12–13.

Osterloh, S., 'Rectifying distributionally regressive microfinance systems in northern Kenya', *Global Livestock CRSP Research Brief* 04-10-PARIMA, 2004.

Sagawa, T., 'Wives' domestic and political activities at home: the space of coffee drinking among the Daasanetch of southwestern Ethiopia', *African Study Monographs*, vol. 27, no. 2, 2006, pp. 63–86.

Sikar, N.K. and Hodgson, D.L., 'In the shadow of the MDGs: pastoralist women and children in Tanzania', *Indigenous Affairs*, no. 1, 2006, pp. 31–7.

Smith, K., 'Sedentarization and market integration: new opportunities for Rendille and Ariaal women of northern Kenya', *Human Organization*, vol. 57, no. 4, 1998, pp. 459–68.

Spencer, P., *The Maasai of Matapato: A Study of Rituals and Rebellion*, Bloomington, Indiana University Press, 1988.

Stites, E., Akabwai, D., Mazurana, D. and Ateyo, P., *Angering Akuju: Survival and Suffering in Karamoja, A Report on Livelihoods and Human Security in the Karamoja Region of Uganda*, Medford, MA, Feinstein International Center, Tufts University, 2007.

Talle, A., 'Pastoralists at the border: Maasai poverty and the development discourse in Tanzania', in D. Anderson and V. Broch-Due (eds), *The Poor Are Not Us: Poverty and Pastoralism in Eastern Africa*, Oxford, James Currey, 1999, pp. 106–24.

Talle, A., '"Serious Games": Licenses and Prohibitions in Maasai Sexual Life', *Africa*, vol. 77, no. 3, 2007, pp. 351–70.

United Nations Convention to Combat Desertification (UNCCD), *Women Pastoralists: Preserving Traditional Knowledge, Facing Modern Challenges*, Bonn, Secretariat of UNCCD and the International Fund for Cooperative Development, 2007.

Watson, C., *Pastoral Women as Peacemakers*, Nairobi, Community Based Animal Health and Participatory Epidemiology Unit of the African Union/Interafrican Bureau for Animal Resources, 2003.

Watson, E., 'Inter-institutional alliances and conflicts in natural resource management: preliminary research findings from Borana, Oromia Region, Ethiopia', *Working Paper 4*, Brighton, Marena Research Project, 2000.

Wawire, V.K., *Gender and the Social and Economic Impacts of Drought on the Residents of Turkana District in Northern Kenya*, Addis Ababa, Organization for Social Science Research in Eastern and Southern Africa (OSSREA), 2003.

Yohannes Gebre Michael, Kassaye Hadgu and Zerihun Ambaye, *Addressing Pastoralist Conflict in Ethiopia: The Case of the Kuraz and Hamer Sub-Districts of South Omo Zone*, Nairobi, Africa Peace Forum, 2005.

Young, J., 'Along Ethiopia's western frontier: Gambella and Benishangul in transition', *Journal of Modern African Studies*, vol. 37, no. 2, 1999, pp. 321–46.